IMAGES OF ENGLA

Leominster

This photograph of the north wall of Leominster Priory was taken early in the twentieth century from the workhouse garden.

IMAGES OF ENGLAND

Leominster

Eric Turton

NONSUCH

West Street, Leominster, at the turn of the twentieth century.

First published 1996
This new pocket edition 2005
Images unchanged from first edition

Nonsuch Publishing Limited
The Mill, Brimscombe Port,
Stroud, Gloucestershire, GL5 2QG
www.nonsuch-publishing.com

British Library Cataloguing in Publication Data.
A catalogue record for this book is available from the British Library.

ISBN 1-84588-156-7

Typesetting and origination by Nonsuch Publishing Limited
Printed in Great Britain by Oaklands Book Services Limited

Contents

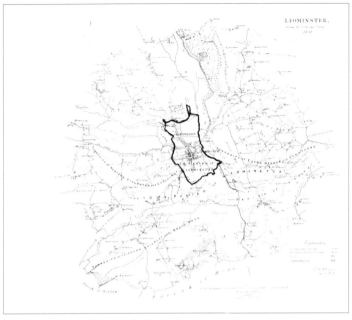

Parliamentary boundary map of 1831 (part).

Church Street, Leominster with(out) figures.

Introduction

It is said that a picture is worth a thousand words, so a combination of words and pictures must be worth even more, and that is what we are presenting here. Some of the pictures will be familiar, possibly because the scene has not changed significantly between the time it was taken and the present day; others show just how much things have altered over the years. The photographs in this book come mainly from the collection in Leominster Museum, both donated and on loan; the remainder has been kindly lent for this publication.

One of the frustrating things about photographs is that far too many are unlabelled so that the 'who', 'when' and 'where' are all unknown. There are often clues for identification and dating in the photographs themselves such as the name over a shop, the name of a licensee, the existence or lack of certain landmarks, but never forget that a photographic image can be misleading or even lie. The photograph of the approaches to the Priory Church (above) shows the photographer (probably Mr Jones) in the process of eliminating all trace of people. I wonder why he gave up? Other photographs are interesting for their contents; the background, the clothes or certain objects like bicycles, wagons, or cars.

Leominster has been fortunate in its photographers, four of them in particular. Two of them, Messrs Jones and Evans, started work in the 1860s. Robert Jones seems to have been the first, working in Leominster until around 1890, while Edward Juson Evans is referred to as 'photographer, grocer and tea-dealer' and seems to have gone into photography as an adjunct to the family grocer's business in South Street. Evans later moved to 22, Burgess Street. T. Henry Winterbourne was the next major Leominster photographer, eventually continuing Robert Jones' business in Broad Street. The fourth was Alfred W. DeAth who took over Evans' premises in Burgess Street and who seems to have taken most of the official photographs in the Borough during the twentieth century.

Right: This view of Robert Jones' premises on Broad Street is a detail from a larger image and was almost certainly taken by Mr Jones, himself, about 1885.

Below left and right: These two photographs were probably not taken by a professional photographer but possibly by Miss Child, eldest daughter of the Leominster station-master. They come from a photograph album which contains a mixture of professional and amateur pictures, the majority of which were taken in and around Leominster around the beginning of the century. Unfortunately, nothing is known about either child, but the photographs are, nevertheless, of considerable interest.

Acknowledgements

As mentioned in the introduction, this book is based largely on the collection of photographs in Leominster Museum. The selection process has been difficult due to the nature of the material available and I hope that it has not been unduly arbitrary.

We wish to take this opportunity to thank all the many people who have helped our collection to grow over the years. One thing that makes it more difficult to mention individually each person whose photograph has been used is the fact that we have up to five copies of some and duplicates of many. However, as Curator of Leominster Museum, I would like to thank especially the Lee family, Mr & Mrs Burlton, the late Mrs Wiseman, and last, but very far from least, Mr Richard Winterbourn whose gift included some very early photographs by his grandfather's predecessor at 36, Broad Street, Robert Jones. Some photographs have been lent especially for this book and I would like to thank Lord Cawley for permission to include the deAth photograph of his grandfather, father, and three uncles; Mr Ian Stair for his imaginative reconstruction of the Priory, and Mrs Maureen Crumpler for the delightful photograph of herself and friends on p. 127.

The ducking stool, one of the few remaining examples that has actually been used, is now kept in the north aisle of the Priory Church (see page 20).

One

What's in a name?

This nineteenth-century view of the Priory from the north, looking across the Kenwater, a branch of the River Lugg, has changed very little apart from the fact that the field has become a car park.

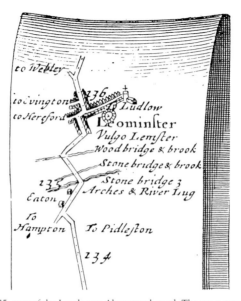

Ogilby map of 1675, part of the London to Aberystwyth road. The most common questions about the town of Leominster relate to the name, its spelling, pronunciation, and meaning. Contrary to some beliefs the spelling has not been significantly changed since Llanllieni (the Welsh name meaning 'the church on the streams') became 'Leomynster'. By the time the first map-makers came around asking the names of towns and villages, the local people pronounced it 'Lemster' and so it was written down. Ogilby got it right when he labels it 'Leominster, vulgo Lemster', but several maps use the colloquial spelling, as do some milestones. Local pronunciation is still 'Lemster'. All sorts of legends have grown up around the meaning of the name, such as the story of Edfride and the lion or that the town was founded by Leofric, earl of Mercia. However, in fact it is simply a corruption/translation into English of the Welsh. The first element, 'Leo', or 'Leon' is also found as 'land' in Monkland, Eardisland, etc. The second element is self-explanatory, for the town owes its existence to the foundation of a monastery in or around the year 660 AD by Merewalh, son of Penda, who was married to a Kentish princess. A Saxon minster was a church serving a large area, and there was probably a Saxon stone building here. The town was sacked by the Welsh on several occasions and the minster and associated monastery or nunnery destroyed. In 1046, Sweyn, brother of Earl (and later King) Harold, on his way back from a successful campaign against the Welsh, ran off with the abbess, Edgiva. According to the story 'he had her as long as he pleased and afterwards let her go home'. Shortly afterwards, the monastery seems to have been abandoned, perhaps following the capture of the town by the Welsh in 1052 when Gruffudd ap Llywelyn invaded the perpetually unstable border area. There is, however, considerable uncertainty about the exact date of this 'dissolution' as although there is no mention of the church in the Domesday Book three priests are referred to. The manors which had been in the possession of the minster are listed as having belonged to Queen Edith. There is, however, far more certainty about the new foundation: this followed the grant of the manor to Reading Abbey in 1123.

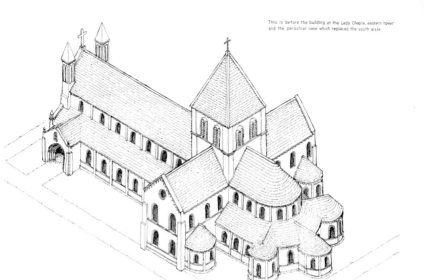

This is before the building of the Lady Chaple, eastern tower and the parochial nave which replaced the south aisle

POSSIBLE APPEARANCE OF LEOMINSTER PRIORY CHURCH IN THE 12th CENTURY

IAN R STAIR Delt 1992

There is no record of the original appearance of the church, but Ian Stair's imaginative reconstruction is based on the available evidence and gives some idea of what it might have looked like. The Priory was dedicated to St Peter and in 1239 the south aisle was replaced by the nave of the parish church which was dedicated to St Paul. An additional nave, or large south aisle, was added in 1320. Unusually, the monastic buildings were to the north of the church, so they were undisturbed by the new additions. They did not remain undisturbed after 1539 when King Henry VIII, in a drive to destroy Roman Catholic monasticism, dissolved the monasteries. The east end of the church with its chapels was pulled down and the stone from this and the cloisters seems to have been used for building materials, some of which have been found in various parts of the town. The inhabitants of Leominster managed to save the church, the chalice, and part of the old Priory buildings. In March 1699 (or 1700 in the new style Gregorian calendar adopted in England in 1752, when New Year's Day was changed from 25 March to 1 January) while workmen were repairing the roof, a fire was started which nearly destroyed the church. Once again the people of Leominster came to the rescue and raised the large sum needed for its restoration.

One of the most splendid features of the Norman building was the doorway with its beautifully carved capitals, both inside and out. This was probably moved when the west tower was built, but it remains one of the glories of the Leominster school of sculpture.

This aerial view shows quite clearly the Priory as it was in 1920, and as it had been for about a century before. The view is taken looking west and shows the Pinsley brook bordering the churchyard on the east and turning due west to pass under the old monastic buildings. These, with nineteenth-century additions, were used as the workhouse until the Second World War. Most of the area visible as far as the gardens at the top of the photograph formed the Priory precinct from Saxon times. The Abbot's fishponds were in the fields (now mainly carpark) below the gasometer which can be seen in the top right-hand corner of the photograph. The building just to the left of the church tower was built as the National School in 1858.

The Priory from the south-east. The porch was rebuilt in the early nineteenth century in a style, according to Revd Jonathan Williams, writing in 1808, 'of the most glaring incongruity, exhibiting a barbarous mixture of two orders of architecture the most opposite to each other'.

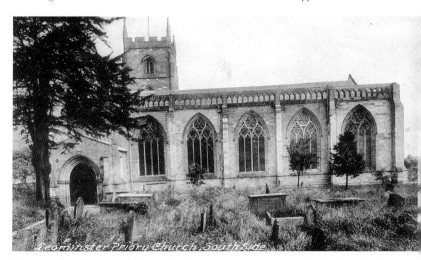

The Priory from the south. Both these late Victorian photographs show the churchyard before the tombs were removed.

Above: This photograph of the Priory interior was taken soon after 1860 and shows a very different view to that visible today. While it is largely as it was left when reopened in 1705 after restoration work, numerous changes had taken place. The first was the erection of a west gallery for the scholars of the new charity school in 1722. This gallery was enlarged in 1737 when an organ was purchased. In 1756 the small gallery in the bottom, left-hand corner of the photograph was built to provide five pews for private subscribers, ownership of which went with various properties in the town. In 1841 the organ, enlarged in 1797, was placed at the east end of the chancel.

Right: The main gallery was erected in 1839–40 and paid for by public subscription, and despite asking for payment to be made before the alterations were begun, reminders were still being written in September 1840.

Leominster, Jan. 31st, 1839.

We take the liberty of requesting you at your earliest convenience to pay your Subscription towards the erection of a Gallery in the Parish Church of Leominster, into the hands of Mr. Thomas J. Woodhouse, Treasurer, or into the Leominster Bank, to his account. It being necessary that the money should be paid before the Alterations are commenced.

We are

Yours Respectfully

RICHARD ABLEY,
JOHN MEREDITH, } *Churchwardens.*

The Leominster Church Restoration Committee

BEG to enclose a Report from Mr. G. G. Scott, on the Old Priory Church or Minster. To this Report they give their entire approval, and trust that the time has arrived, when, after a lapse of 800 years, that venerable edifice in which generations have worshipped,—and under the shadow of which they rest in hope,—may be restored to the full use for which it was erected, and to His Glory to whom it was first dedicated.

The Inhabitants as well as Land and Tithe Owners of the district of which Leominster is the centre, may fairly be expected to take an interest in the proposed undertaking, and the Committee therefore hope that each, according to his means, will help to further a work, utterly beyond the power of the Parishioners to accomplish unaided.

Much of the proposed outlay, which it is estimated will be about £10,000, is, as will appear from Mr. Scott's Report, *absolutely necessary.* Accommodation for 1,800 persons will be provided by the alterations, and to many now compelled for want of room to seek religious instruction elsewhere, the opportunity will be afforded of offering up their prayers, and hearing the word of life in the Church of their Fathers.

If rich and poor would, for the time the work of Restoration is going on, *(a period of about five years),* devote a portion of their substance to this object, the whole of the proposed Restorations might easily be effected.

COMMITTEE:

The Rev. AUGUSTIN G. EDOUART, *Vicar.*

Mr. WILLIAM GILKES,
  ,, H. N. EDWARDS, } *Churchwardens.*

JOHN H. ARKWRIGHT, Esq.	Mr. ALDERMAN BURLTON.
ELIAS CHADWICK, Esq.	Mr. ALDERMAN STALLARD
ROBERT LANE, Esq.	Mr. ALDERMAN BEDFORD.
The Venerable Archdeacon LANE FREER, D.D.	
The Rev. J. F. CROUCH, *Rural Dean.*	THOMAS SALE, Esq.
The Rev. G. T. WHITFIELD.	HENRY MOORE, Esq.
The Rev. EDWARD C. EVANS.	EDWIN LLOYD, Esq.
CAPT. TURNER.	

The Committee earnestly solicit Contributions either by *Donations* or *Annual Subscriptions,* the extent of which may be notified upon the enclosed form, which may be forwarded to the Reverend the VICAR, or to Mr. H. GAMBLE, the Honorary Secretary.

Leominster, August 1st, 1862.

[TURN OVER.]

The new vicar, the Revd A.G. Edouart, was appalled by the state of the church when he first arrived in Leominster in 1862. Apart from general neglect, the Norman nave was covered in soil, partly from the vaults underneath, entirely burying the bases of the Norman columns. The arcade on the south side of the nave had been built up with masonry and the church was thickly coated with plaster and whitewash. After a public meeting in May 1862, a restoration committee was appointed and the restoration of the Norman nave was commenced in May 1864, under the supervision of Sir Gilbert Scott RA.

The Norman nave. Having been unusable for many years it was the first part of the Priory to be restored, and it was used, as shown, for worship from 1866 while the main nave was being partly reconstructed.

The north side of the church. The cloister and monastic buildings were here until the dissolution. This was the front garden of the workhouse when the photograph was taken.

The restoration committee not only restored the Norman nave but extended the north aisle to the east, adding an additional window. It is in this north aisle that the ducking stool is housed. Made in 1718 to replace an earlier model, it was designed to punish wrongdoers and was used for a final time in 1809 to 'duck' Jenny Pipes, the last person in England to suffer this humiliation.

View taken during the restoration of the south nave between 1876 and 1879. The holes in the wall below the window on the right show where the gallery had been removed.

During the latter stages of restoration the organ seems to have found a temporary resting-place in the north aisle.

The rest of the church was restored in stages, being completed in 1880. The galleries had been removed and the pillars between the central and southern naves completely reformed. The box-pews, referred to by Revd Edouart as being more like sheep-pens, had vanished.

It is interesting to compare this photograph with that on page 17. As well as the changes mentioned above, the organ has been moved from in front of the east window to the south nave, and the screen has been added, together with a fine new ceiling.

Leominster Priory Church choir, *c.* 1910. Among the members are: Jack Jones, Laurie Harris, Jack Rawlings, ? Downes, Cecil Grubb, Reg Hughes, ? Penny, ? Vernalls, ? Elesmere, S. Davies, C. Armitage, Revd F.P.P. Harvey, Revd E.E. Charles, ? Jones (schoolmaster), ? Mayer (organist), Henry Bays, J. Harrison, W. Pennell, W.G. Beaman, Ben Badham, W. Bradford, H.E. Crimp (choirmaster), J.H. Stanley, Charlie Turner, J. Firth, Vincent Coates, Ted Owen, Jack Johnson, ? Owen, Reg Harris, J.H. Carwardine, ? Stafford, Bert Smith, Andres Robinson, Boyd Smith, Bert Jones. The choir had remained largely unsung until in 1863 it became the subject of letters to the *Hereford Times* (e.g. on 18 July 1863) and was dragged into a curious exchange of printed pamphlets involving the curate, the vicar, and the Curate's Fund Committee. The choir had resigned, according to Revd Edouart, or had been sacked, according to the choir, together with the organist. Fortunately, the choir survived as these photographs show.

Leominster Priory Church choir, 1923 on the occasion of the 'egg and flower service'. Members include: D. Waldron, J. Clingo, Robert Adcock, Bert Harvey, Fred Bassett, ? Anthony, Sidney Clingo, Reg Bishop, Leslie Hicks, Bert Beal, ? Anthony, Bill Beal, Reg Ladd, Stanley Harvey.

Left: The new organ at Leominster Prioy Church which was dedicated and opened on 18 December 1924.

Below: Some of those present at the dedication of the new organ in 1924. From left to right, back row: Messrs F.A. Dalley and C.H. Harvey (churchwardens), H.E. Crump (organist and choirmaster), W.C. Jones and S.A. Wilshere (Messrs Nicholson & Co. Ltd, organ builders). Front row: Professor J.D. Bridge, Mus. Doc., FSA, Revd R. Gillenders MA, MC (vicar), Mr W.St.G. Drennan (Hon. Secretary).

Two

Grange Court:
the life and adventures of a
building

An enlarged portion of Galliers' map of 1825.

Abel's Market House as he designed it. In the early years of the seventeenth century Leominster was a prosperous town and its council decided it was time to replace the old Market-House at the Butter Cross with something more in keeping with the town's growing importance. The Butter Cross is in the centre of the town where five streets meet, one of which is the street leading to the Priory. It is the most prominent site in the town, and the new building was to be plainly visible from three of the streets. To design and build the new building the council chose John Abel, the most prominent local architect, later to be given the honorary title of 'King's Carpenter' by King Charles I for his services during the siege of Hereford. Abel was born in 1577 in Sarnesfield, some ten miles outside Leominster on the road to Brecon. He was a Roman Catholic and would have seen the head of Father Cadwallader (hanged, drawn and quartered at the Iron Cross in the centre of Leominster in 1610) decorating the building he was hired to replace. The new building he erected in 1633 had an open arcade at street level with a chamber over it and attics in the roof lit by four dormer windows. It was decorated with numerous carved figures and the coats of arms of the subscribers who made its erection possible, together with a number of inscriptions, mostly in Latin. These Latin inscriptions were Abel's trade-mark, appearing in the church at Vowchurch, the Town Hall at Brecon, Monnington Court, and many other of his buildings.

At this time the Town Council met in the Frere Chamber over the Priory gateway which spanned Church Street just west of the Forbury chapel. In 1750 the council decided to move, so the Market-House was refurbished and the main chamber divided into two to serve as both court and council chamber. In 1752 the old Priory gateway with the Frere Chamber fell down, taking part of the gaol with it.

The Old Town Hall, (Now Grange Court) Leominster.

The Old Town Hall after the weight of the roof had been reduced. By the 1790s the increase in wheeled traffic in the town led to complaints that the Town Hall was blocking the entrance to the High Street. When it was heard that the council proposed to improve the stability of the building mainly by lessening the weight of its roof, an open letter was circulated proposing its removal and re-erection in Corn Square. The letter was largely ignored and the Town Hall was instead modified. The four dormers were removed and the stone tiles replaced with slates, thus creating the roof we can see today. In 1808 the Leominster Enclosure Act was passed. This included elaborate plans for improving the streets of Leominster and the buildings, or parts of them, that caused obstructions and which were to be moved are listed at the end of the Act. An attempt to get the Town Hall included was thwarted mainly by the 11th Duke of Norfolk, who owned a house in Etnam Street and was very active in local politics. This annoyed the Revd Jonathan Williams, headmaster of the grammar school, who did not hesitate to say so in his book, *The Leominster Guide*, published in 1808, referring to 'the interference of the noble representative of the most ancient dukedom in the kingdom'.

This photograph, almost certainly taken in 1860 or very soon after, is the only one to show Grange Court without its adjourning conservatory.

By the middle of the nineteenth century, the town needed both a larger covered market and a more commodious town hall so, in 1854, a number of properties in the High Street and Burgess Street were purchased and then auctioned as building materials. With the building of a new town hall on this site the Old Town Hall not only became redundant but blocked the entrance to the new building. Mr Edward Russell was instructed to auction the Town Hall on 30 April 1855, before it was pulled down. The bidding started at £50 and the building was finally knocked out to Mr Francis Davis, druggist, for the sum of £95. Mr Davis, whose shop was at 2, High Street, was the younger brother of John Scarlett Davis, the Leominster painter. The event was considered of sufficient importance to be reported, with an illustration, in the Illustrated London News for 12 May 1855. Some of the inhabitants of Leominster, dismayed by the impending disappearance of a well-loved building, asked the Mayor to call a meeting to determine its future. In the meantime the Old Town Hall had been sold by Mr Davis to John Arkwright, Esq., of Hampton Court, also for £95, and he offered it to the town if a suitable use and location for its re-erection could be found. At the meeting a committee was formed to carry this out, and at the next council meeting it was agreed that the best site would be Corn Square. The centre of the square was occupied by a stone building built in 1808 that served as the Corn Market. It was decided that this building should be sold to the Old Town Hall Committee for a nominal sum so that it could be demolished. The committee began collecting subscriptions to pay for the demolition and re-erection and the Old Town Hall was dismantled in August, 1855. At the next council meeting, however, they decided that the Corn Market should remain, only six feet at one end being sold to the committee so that the Old Town Hall could be built transversely at the end of the Corn Market. There was considerable opposition to all this for various reasons, even to the choice of use for the old building as a library, reading-room and museum; one councillor objected that it 'may be used for purposes that are very objectionable to the town' without specifying what. The council changed its mind again and sold the Corn Market by auction on 25 November 1855 for building materials. Then, on 5 February 1856, a letter was received threatening legal proceedings if the building was re-erected 'in such a manner as to stand upon or cover any part of the said ground hitherto not built upon or in such a manner as to interfere or impede the passage across or through the said Square and public thoroughfare'. This was rather unexpected for the writer had subscribed to the re-erection of the Town Hall in Corn Square. The whole project ground to a halt. Later, Mr Arkwright purchased five plots of land adjoining the Grange and had the Old Town Hall re-erected in 1858-9 as a private dwelling, the ground-floor arcade being filled in and the building considerably extended at the back.

TO ADMIRERS OF
ANTIQUITY.

TOWN-HALL,
Leominster, Herefordshire
MR. E. RUSSELL

Has received instructions from the Town Council of the Borough of Leominster to offer for

PUBLIC COMPETITION,
ON THE PREMISES,
On Monday, the 30th April, 1855,
AT TWELVE O'CLOCK AT NOON;
THAT MUCH-ADMIRED OLD BUILDING, CALLED
THE TOWN-HALL,
SITUATE IN THE CENTRE OF THE TOWN.

This is One of the few remaining Timber Structures of the 16th Century; it was erected by John Abel, the most noted Architect of his time. It is composed of Timber and Plaster, and adorned with curious Grotesque Figures, in a good state of preservation, standing on 12 Oak Pillars of the Old Ionic Order, now sustained on Stone Pedestals. The upper part of the Building displays a profusion of Carving, and various Sentences are inscribed upon it.

To all Lovers of such curious antiquated Buildings, an opportunity of gratifying their tastes now presents itself, which may never occur again, and which should not be lost sight of.

☞ Further Particulars may be obtained of Mr. THOMAS SALE, Town Clerk, Leominster.

LEOMINSTER. FRANCIS WENT. PRINTER. HIGH-STREET.

Does anyone want to buy an old Town Hall?

Left: The Moore family at play, Grange Court, *c.* 1861. *Right:* Map from the 1907 Grange Court sale catalogue.

LOT 11.

Coloured Pink on Plan.   Number on Ordnance Sheet, Part 176.

All that Beautifully Timbered and Historical Residence,

Known as

The Grange Court House,

SITUATE AT THE GRANGE.

The house stands in its own grounds, and contains dining room, 18ft. 6in. by 17ft. 6in. by 13ft. 6in. high; morning room, 14ft. by 14ft. by 9ft. 6in. high; study, 16ft. 6in. by 11ft. 3in. by 12ft. 6in. high; drawing room, 20ft. by 17ft. 3in. by 11ft. high; 7 bedrooms, bathroom, w.c., and usual domestic offices; walled-in garden with vineries and conservatory, good stabling and coach-house.

This ancient residence was originally built by John Abel, the renowned architect of King Charles I., and has remarkable mottoes on the North, South and West sides.

It is in the occupation of W. Kostin, Esq., and near to the centre of the town, church, and railway station. The acreage is 0a. 2r. 39., and it is let at the annual rent of £65.

The Land Tax is 19s. 4d.

The intermediate land between the boundary of this lot and the Grange is the property of the Ecclesiastical Commissioners, for the enjoyment of which an acknowledgment of £1 per annum is paid.

The lean-to portable Kennels with the iron railings belong to the tenant.

Description from the 1907 Grange Court sale catalogue. Mr Arkwright never lived there but rented the property to Mr Henry Moore, a local solicitor, until all the Arkwright property in Leominster was put up for auction in 1907. Only two bids (of £700 and £800) were received and the lot was withdrawn, to be sold privately to Theodore Neild, Esq., a Quaker.

One sunny day in May, 1909, a large number of Leominster citizens, dressed in their best, gathered on the Grange. This was a favourite pastime, but more were there than usual because they had come to see how badly Grange Court had been damaged by fire.

Contents on the lawn, Grange Court, 1909. See the letter at the bottom of the next page.

After he purchased Grange Court, Theodore Neild had commissioned Mr Storr Barber, a local builder who was also a sculptor, to restore the building. This he did very well and two sculptured portraits of Mr Neild were incorporated: one in a lozenge on the south end of the building and one in the ceiling of the lobby. Unfortunately, as the work was coming to an end on the restoration of the roof, a careless workman set fire to it. Thanks to the fire brigade led by Mr J. Budd and other helpers the damage was confined to the roof. Storr Barber, probably the gentleman on the ladder below the fireman, had a narrow escape when a stone tile fell on his head as he was carrying an empty bucket down the ladder. Mr Neild wrote the following letter of thanks to the *Leominster News* on 27 May 1909:

'To the Editor, Sir:- May I, through you, most warmly thank all who, either officially or unofficially, laboured last Monday [24 May 1909] to save the work of John Abel, of John Arkwright, and – I cannot refrain from adding – of Storr Barber, from the flames? The efforts made were such as only those could exert who felt that a public heirloom was at stake. All other claims, risk of personal injury, and even danger to life were disregarded, whilst appliance of every kind and neighbourly help (with abundant offers of more) were placed at our disposal. The knowledge that public spirit prompted some of the most efficient service does not lessen the gratitude we feel to every helper. For it would have been an abiding sorrow to think that a building which nearly three centuries had so tenderly treated had been destroyed while in our care. We are very happy to find that no one was seriously hurt, and also that so little that was historic has suffered. Few of the lighter timbers burned were from the original structure. Some of the old main timbers may perhaps be kept. It is to be regretted, of course, that most of the stone tiles and crests, which had been finely mellowed by the 50 years spent on the roof since they came out of Hampton Court quarry, cannot be used again. Lastly, may I thank all who so quickly and carefully, as a precaution, emptied the house, or who took any share in the prompt refilling.'

Theodore Neild and his wife, Helen Newman Neild on their day of their Diamond wedding anniversary in 1928.

A Leominster banknote, showing the Town Hall, symbol for the town, in the centre. After Mr Neild's death, Grange Court was bought by the Baker family, but in February 1937, soon after Mr Baker's death, attention was drawn at a meeting of the Leominster Chamber of Commerce to the fact that it was up for sale and might be removed from the district. The property had been offered to the council by the trustees of the estate of the late owner, but they considered the price too high, so its sale to an American was being negotiated. The council acted quickly and a preservation order was made on 23 March 1937 and confirmed by the Ministry of Health on 19 May. This prohibited its demolition but led to a demand from the owners for £2,000 compensation as the preservation order had decreased the value of the property. The matter went to arbitration and in June 1937, the owners were awarded a total of £1,583. The council then negotiated the purchase of the property which was completed in 1939. The building then became council offices, which it remains today.

Three

'Confound their politics'

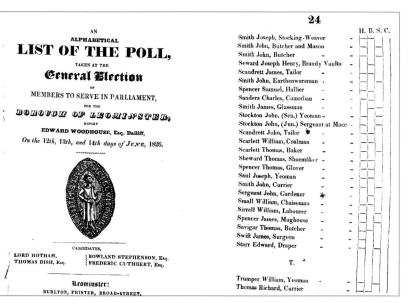

24

	H.	B.	S.	C.
Smith Joseph, Stocking-Weaver	-			
Smith John, Butcher and Mason	-			
Smith John, Butcher	-			
Seward Joseph Henry, Brandy Vaults	-			
Scandrett James, Tailor	-			
Smith John, Earthenwareman	-			
Spencer Samuel, Hallier	-			
Sanders Charles, Comedian	-			
Smith James, Glassman	-			
Stockton John, (Sen.) Yeoman	-			
Stockton John, (Jun.) Sergeant at Mace	-			
Scandrett John, Tailor	-			
Scarlett William, Coalman	-			
Scarlett Thomas, Baker	-			
Sheward Thomas, Shoemaker	-			
Spencer Thomas, Glover	-			
Saul Joseph, Yeoman	-			
Smith John, Currier	-			
Sergeant John, Gardener	*			
Small William, Chaiseman	-			
Sirrell William, Labourer	-			
Spencer James, Mughouse	-			
Savigar Thomas, Butcher	-			
Swift James, Surgeon	-			
Starr Edward, Draper	-			
T.				
Trumper William, Yeoman	-			
Thomas Richard, Currier	-			

This excerpt from the 'List of the Poll' taken on three days in June 1826 serves to remind us of several things: that Leominster returned two members to parliament; that there was no secret ballot; that only men had the vote; that an unexpectedly wide range of people held the franchise.

	H. B. S. C.
Williams George, Dyer -	
Wormington William, Yeoman	
Williams John, Hoopshaver ✳	
Williams Richard, Servant -	
Weaver William, Carpenter ✳	
Whimberry Benjamin, Rag-gatherer	
Wharburton Richard, Mason ✳	
Walter Thomas, (Lodging House) ✳	
Watling Thomas F, Surgeon -	
Wood John, Carpenter	
Watcham Thomas, Jockey -	
Williams Thomas, Leatherdresser ✳	
Woodward Henry, Draper -	
Wood James, Joiner -	

ABSTRACT OF THE NUMBERS POLLED.

	H.	B.	S.	C.
Hotham and Bish	314	314		
Hotham and Stephenson	179		179	
Hotham and Cuthbert	19			19
Bish and Stephenson		63	63	
Bish and Cuthbert		34		34
Stephenson and Cuthbert			3	3
Single Votes	45	34	9	1
Total for each Candidate	557	445	254	57

Total Number Polled .... 701.

Leominster sent two members to Parliament from 1295 until the Reform Act of 1867 reduced it to one. It was not a 'pocket borough' so, for much of that time, candidates or their patrons had to buy votes, and Leominster achieved the doubtful honour of being one of the most expensive in the kingdom. Sir George Caswell, in fact, was accused of paying £20 per vote and was actually taken to task for it, his election in 1717 being declared void for that reason. However, the electors of Leominster simply voted him in again. As we shall see in a later chapter they did the same after he had been expelled from the House of Commons in 1721. The published list of the 1826 poll, housed in Leominster Museum, has a note inside the back cover showing how much each of the candidates owed the voters, about £6 per vote.

TO THE
Electors of the Borough
OF
Leominster.

GENTLEMEN,

       YOU may rely upon it that the Third Candidate now brought forward is one of those who wish to wring from the Poor Man as much of his hard-earned wages as they can without driving him to absolute despair,—depend upon it, he is a Supporter of all the oppressive Acts of the present Min-s--y, he is one of those who wish to make the Shilling Loaf (already far too small), even smaller than it is, he would give the money which is drawn from your pockets to those men who have been already marked out by the public abhorrence, as *Drones* who live on "the fat of that land" which they do not contribute to support —And above all, consider that he is a *Scotchman*. That he is a Native of that Country famed for *avarice* and *cunning*. I do not ask you to vote for your Old Members, I only wish you to recollect that if you vote for this man, you might as well have voted for Sir J. G. C——, they support the same measures, and if you refuse him who is a Native of your County, and has represented you in Parliament, how much more ought you to do so by this proud Scotchman who scarcely looks down on you whilst he solicits your Votes.

A VOTER.

April 25, 1818.

F. J. BURLTON, PRINTER.

Candidates were often elected and then unseated for a variety of reasons. The literature produced at the 1818 election was not particularly insulting, but a lot was made of the fact that one of the candidates, Sir W. Cunningham Fairley, a Tory, was also a Scotsman. This was eventually the reason for him being unseated for as his property was in Scotland it could not be counted for the property qualification essential for any English MP. The law was changed and he was duly elected in 1820.

'3 o'clock and a fine morning' by Gilray. The duke of Norfolk (right) with a bottle of port in his pocket and Sheridan, the politician (left) leaving Brook's Club in London. One of the most important elements in English politics was the influence of patrons. These were frequently people who, having had a seat in the Commons, had inherited a peerage and wanted someone to represent their interests in the lower house. Earl Coningsby was one such, his chosen candidate being Sir George Caswell. Another peer who attempted to get his chosen candidate elected in Leominster was the 11th duke of Norfolk. As the earl of Surrey he had played an important part in the House of Commons, being one of those who forced Lord North's resignation, and he owned property in Leominster, notably Norfolk House in Etnam Street. A quarrel with a rival candidate's patron, Lord Viscount Malden (heir to the earl of Essex and owner of Hampton Court near Leominster) over, among other things, the provision by the duke's agent of several hogheads of cider for the voters of Leominster after announcing that 'dinner was ready', led to them fighting a duel. This was reported in the Gentleman's Magazine on Saturday 30 April:

'In consequence of a publication addressed by Lord Malden to the inhabitants of the borough of Leominster, the Duke of Norfolk, accompanied by Capt. Wombwell, of the First West York Regiment of Militia (of which the duke was Colonel), and Lord Malden, accompanied by Capt. Taylor, Aid de Camp to his Royal Highness the Duke of York, met on Saturday evening in a field beyond Paddington. The parties having taken their ground, and the word being given by one of the seconds, they fired without effect. The seconds then thought proper to offer their interference, and, in consequence of a conversation which passed while the parties were on the ground, a reconciliation was effected.'

I am surprised anyone could miss the duke, he made a large enough target and, as the illustration clearly shows, he made splendid subject material (above) for Gilray the political cartoonist.

Edmund Lamb, Liberal MP for North Herefordshire (1906–1910).

Another type of patronage had come into play in early nineteenth-century Leominster when the eldest son of the 1st Viscount Melbourne died and his lordship wanted a suitable seat for his new heir, William Lamb. Fortunately, one of the Leominster MPs, Charles Kinnaird, had just inherited a peerage so his seat was made available. It is not recorded whether William's wife of seven months, Lady Caroline Lamb, came down with him for the election. (Byron, her lover, actually had another mistress in the Leominster area, the Countess of Oxford, mother of the 'Harlean miscellany', several children by different fathers, but then again William Lamb was probably not his father's son.)

At Leominster, there were also frequent petitions to declare particular elections invalid, such as that mentioned in the case of Sir Cunningham Fairley and after the 1826 election when Thomas Bish was found to hold a position of profit under the Crown – in this case he was a national lottery contractor. Bish was replaced by Rowland Stephenson who, in turn, lost his seat when he ran off to the United States with money from the banking house of Remington, Stephenson & Co., and was declared an outlaw!

Edmund Lamb's election headquarters. Leominster managed to hold on to its two seats in the first Reform Act of 1831, but it lost one in the second Reform Act of 1867, and the second in the Redistribution of Seats Act of 1885. The Conservative MP at this time was James Rankin (later Sir James) who, with two exceptions, was to win every election for North Herefordshire until 1912. In 1885 and again in 1906 the Liberal Party was victorious and on the latter occasion the successful candidate was Edmund G. Lamb. He lost his seat in January 1910 and was replaced as Liberal candidate by Wyatt Paine. The Liberal headquarters was Grafton House, then next to the New Inn which is now the exit from the central car park.

Opposite above: Wyatt Paine in his car.

Opposite below: Paine's headquarters.

Left: Sir James Rankin. He was succeeded as Conservative member for North Herefordshire by Henry Fitzherbert Wright who was elected at a 'bye-election' in March 1912. This was just a month after the Rankin Constitutional Club had been opened in Corn Square, from an upper window of which Wright thanked the electors after the declaration of the result.

Below: Mr Fitzherbert Wright thanking electors for his victory in 1912.

Four

The Great Houses of
Leominster district

Croft Castle from the west, showing one of the magnificent trees in the park.

The nearest stately home to Leominster is Berrington Hall. Berrington was the home of the Cornewall (sometimes spelled Cornwall) family from medieval times, but in 1787 it was purchased by Thomas Harley, third son of the 3rd earl of Oxford. He was a banker and government contractor who had been Lord Mayor of London in 1767. He was also a Member of Parliament, first for London and then for Herefordshire. The architect was Henry Holland and the park was laid out by Capability Brown, Holland's father-in-law. The rather faded photograph above was probably taken in the 1880s and is one of the few to show the Rodney cannon, captured by Admiral Rodney from the Spaniards. The Rodney connection came about because in 1781 Thomas Harley's second daughter, Ann, had married George, the eldest son of Admiral Rodney, who was a friend of Harley. George became the 2nd Lord Rodney in 1792, but died in 1802, two years before his father-in-law. It was his wife, Ann, who thus inherited the house from her father, whose only son, Edward, had died in 1768 at the age of eleven. She was succeeded by three of her sons in turn, each of whom died without male issue, and then by the son of her fourth son. He was the 7th Lord Rodney and inherited the title in 1864 when he was seven years old.

Berrington Hall from the pool. Capability Brown was fond of water and this photograph was taken from the island in the middle of the lake he created. Although it is almost fourteen acres in extent, he insisted on calling it a 'pool'. The house faces south-west across a lawn bordered by a 'ha-ha' and there were also tennis and croquet lawns, flower beds, shrubberies, a rosery and two large walled-in kitchen gardens. The island in the pool is now a heronry. The house, itself, was supplied by water both from the hills and from a well in the courtyard. This and the following photograph were taken during the final years of the Rodneys at Berrington, c. 1890.

The staircase hall at Berrington during the Victorian period. Note the contrast between the rather plain exterior and the beautiful interior design and decor by Henry Holland. Note, also, the paraffin lamps. The pictures to the left and right are two of those depicting Admiral Rodney's victories. They now hang in the dining room.

In January 1891, George Bridges Harley Dennett, 7th Lord Rodney, married the Hon. Corisande Evelyn Vere Guest, second daughter of Lord Wimborne, and grand-daughter of the Duke of Marlborough, at St James's Church, Piccadilly. The occasion was celebrated at Berrington with, among other things, a bonfire and unlimited cider and beer. About thirty elderly women from the estate were regaled with a 'knife-and-fork tea'. After a honeymoon spent in Uxbridge and Brampton Bryan they returned home to an enthusiastic welcome, first in Leominster, and then at Berrington Hall as shown above. In the photograph, Captain Gunnell of the Leominster Volunteers (founded by his lordship's father) can be seen presenting an address of welcome. 'Enclosed in a handsome album the address had been beautifully illuminated by Messrs Thos. De la Rue and Co., and had been greatly admired.' Almost hidden behind Lady Rodney is the white-bearded figure of John Hungerford Arkwright, Chief Steward of the Borough of Leominster and soon to become Lord Lieutenant of Herefordshire. To the right of Captain Gunnell is W.T. Sale the Town Clerk, the Mayor and most of the members of the Corporation of Leominster with their wives. The estate workers and tenantry stood outside, frequently in the rain, together with members of the Leominster fire brigade. The motto 'Home Sweet Home' had been provided by Mr C. Blomer who had just completed the addition of a tower, at the rear of the hall, containing bathrooms and additional stabling for breeding race-horses. Within ten years, however, his lordship had run off with the governess of his four sons and the estate had been sold. His wife divorced him in 1902 and he then married the governess.

On 6 March, 1900 an order-to-view was given to Mr F. Cawley MP which described Berrington Hall as follows: 'Herefordshire (about 1 mile of a railway station, under 3 miles of a market town and 7 of another, with express train service to Liverpool, Manchester, Cardiff and London). To be Sold at a moderate price, a most important Country Seat, comprising about 2,750 acres. The mansion, which stands on an eminence in a well-timbered park of about 400 acres, is built of stone and is approached by 2 drives, guarded by outer lodges and thence through fine iron gates between a handsome double lodge. The porch, gained by a wide flight of stone steps, is supported by stone pillars, and the whole building is of a dignified appearance. It contains on the ground floor, the round or marble hall, inner hall with domed light from which ascends the grand staircase. The magnificent suite of reception rooms comprise ante room, dining room (29ft. 6in. by 21ft. 6in.), billiard room (30ft. by 21ft. 6in.), noble drawing room (35ft. by 23 ft. 9in.), boudoir, morning room, smoking room, &c. The chimney-pieces of these rooms are very elegant marble, the doors of polished mahogany, the ceilings hand-painted with rich designs, and the decorations are in excellent order. The halls are heated with hot water coils. The bed room accommodation on the first floor comprises 4 best bed rooms with dressing rooms and clothes room attached, 3 other bed rooms, bath room fitted hot and cold, and lavatories. On the second floor, approached by a back staircase, with door on to first floor landing are 7 bed rooms, large servants' dormitory, box room, housemaid's pantry, lavatories, &c. The domestic offices are exceedingly well arranged, and comprise house-keeper's room, still room, butler's pantry and bed room, servants hall, large kitchen, scullery, larders, lamp room, &c. There are large cellars for wood, coal, wine, beer and cider, etc.'

The Cawley family came originally from Cheshire and were involved in the cotton industry in Lancashire. Mr Cawley bought the Berrington estate and moved there with his wife and four sons. They are pictured above in 1908 about to go out with the Christmas hunt. From left to right: Oswald Cawley on 'Colonel', Harold Cawley on 'Trivia', Sir F. Cawley, Bart. on 'Scout', John Cawley on 'Dragon', and Robert Cawley on 'Moonstone'. Mr F. Cawley had been elected to parliament in 1895 and was created a baronet in 1906. He was a member of the cabinet from 1916 until January 1918, when he was created Baron Cawley. The life of the family was, however shattered by the First World War; at the beginning of September 1918 the following appeared in the *Leominster News*: 'We deeply regret to state that a report has been received to the effect that the body of Captain Oswald Cawley, whom we reported as wounded and missing last week, has been found and buried. By his death Lord and Lady Cawley have lost their third son in the war, only the eldest, who is engaged in his father's business enterprises, being left to them. The deepest sympathy of local people will go out to them in the further crushing blow which has fallen upon them. The death of Captain Oswald Cawley creates a vacancy in the Prestwich Division of South East Lancashire, of which he was elected member in January by a majority of over 6,000, upon the elevation of his father to the peerage. Captain Cawley was then on military service in Palestine, but took his seat in the House in June. His brother, Major J.S. Cawley was killed at Nery in 1914; and Captain Harold T. Cawley, M.P. for Heywood, fell at Gallipoli in 1915. It is a coincidence that each of the deaths was reported in the month of September. The third (and present) Lord Cawley made Berrington Hall and park over to the National Trust in 1957.

An unusual view of Hampton Court taken from the hill behind the house. John Hungerford Arkwright, the white-bearded gentleman who appears on the porch at Berrington Hall to welcome the bride and groom, was one of the largest land-owners in north Herefordshire possessing the magnificent house of Hampton Court. Not the one near London, of course, but an older one a few miles south of Leominster. The original house was built in the reign of Henry IV by Sir Rowland Lenthall, who married a relative of the king and thus received the estate. The Coningsby family bought the house in the reign of Henry VI and they continued to live there until the end of the eighteenth century. One of the most famous (notorious?) members of that family was the first Earl Coningsby (1657–1729) who is reputed to be the last man in England to employ a jester. He was given his title by William III and the blood-stained handkerchief which he used to staunch the blood from the wound King William received at the battle of the Boyne used to be kept in the house. He was married at the age of seventeen to the daughter of Ferdinando Gorges, a notorious slaver called the 'King of the Blacks', who built Eye Manor. Coningsby seems to have been frequently at odds with his neighbours, sometimes claiming their property, and engaged in endless arguments over the Manor of Leominster which he had purchased, unaware that a lot of the property had been sold off. In 1721, he was imprisoned in the Tower of London accused of insulting the House of Lords, where he was joined by his political protégé, Sir George Caswall, MP for Leominster, put there for his part in the financial scandal of the South Sea Bubble.

The falls at Hampton Court in late Victorian times.

Earl Coningsby's only son died from choking on a cherry stone, so the property passed through the female line to the earl of Essex and was then sold to Richard Arkwright, son of Sir Richard Arkwright of cotton fame. It then passed to his eldest son, John, who considerably enlarged the estate, later inherited by John Hungerford (Squire) Arkwright (above), who became Lord Lieutenant in 1892.

LONG LIFE TO THE
YOUTHFUL HEIR OF
HAMPTON COURT.

Welcome ! sweet babe of Hampton Court,
  In memory of this day we all rejoice,
For surely it is a most happy day,
  Let us lift an unanimous voice.
The house of Hampton Court so bold
  In sweet annals it stands forth ;
Aloud let this joyful tale be told,
  There's a son and heir to a man of such worth.

CHORUS.

Let us at the present moment,
    With one heart and voice declare,
Our wishes for the happiness
    Of Squire Arkwright's son and heir.

Did you see the road from Leominster ?
  Flags and banners flying gay,
Did you see the folks from Walton ?
  To Hampton Court making their way ;
Did you see the sights at Dinmore, ?
  All bedeck'd with flowers rare,
And little children give their welcome,
  To Squire Arkwright's son and heir.

Did you see the grand procession
  Headed by Leominster Rifle band ?
Follow'd by the Odd-fellows,
  Along with the Noble Grand ;

The Foresters next you will see,
  Are the next to follow on,
Did you see bold Robin Hood,
  Along with his friend Little John.

Did you see the fine fat oxen ?
  Drawn in waggons to be sure,
For while the Gents they feast themselves,
  You see they've not forgot the poor.
To those gentlemen great praise is due,
  For subscribing for this eventful time,
Yes, it was my forefathers custom, boys,
  And so it shall be mine.

So now my song is drawing near,
  I wish you all this day much joy,
To Squire Arkwright and his lady,
  And long life to their youthful boy ;
For on this day the bells are ringing,
  And likewise you'll see different sport,
This day will long remembered be,
  For the birth of an Heir at Hampton Court.

London :—H. SUCH, Machine Printer & Publisher, 177, Union Street, Borough. S. E.

This poem celebrates the birth of John Stanhope Arkwright, eldest son of John Hungerford Arkwright, born in 1872. He became both an MP and a poet.

The east frontage of Croft Castle, before the addition of the porch in 1913. The oldest of the stately homes in the area, this has been the home of the Croft family from Domesday to the present day, with one significant gap (1746–1923). An erstwhile border castle, it was converted into a country house in 1765, when it was owned by the Johnes family.

A photograph of Croft Church from the turn of the twentieth century.

The south and west fronts of Croft Castle, after the modifications made in 1913.

This rare photograph, taken about 1900, also shows how the castle looked before the 1913 modifications when the battlements and crow-stepped gables were removed from the south front, together with the small porch on the left.

Oak-panelled bedroom at Croft Castle. When the castle was sold at the beginning of this century the sales catalogue gave some interesting glimpses into the parts of the castle the public does not normally see.

A bathroom at Croft Castle. The National Trust took over the freehold of the castle in 1957 although members of the Croft family still live there, thus ensuring the continuity of the long family association.

Shobdon Court, the home of the Bateman family, was only a few miles west of Croft Castle. Built in the eighteenth century, the main building was pulled down in 1933. This Victorian photograph shows the west front with, possibly, Lady Bateman on horseback.

FROM

THE RIGHT HON. LORD BATEMAN,

WITH HIS LORDSHIP'S GRATEFUL THANKS,

To Mr. J. Monnington.

For his Assistance and Exertions in preserving

SHOBDON COURT MANSION

From destruction by Fire, on December 7th, 1888.

A late Victorian view of Burton Court, a fascinating mixture of everything from medieval to Sir Clough Williams Ellis, open to the public and well worth a visit, both for the house and for the collection of costumes it contains.

Buckland Hall, near Docklow, one of the many other large houses in the Leominster area.

Buckland, at the end of the nineteenth century.

58

Puddleston Court, a few miles east of Leominster, photographed here around 1900. It was built for the Chadwick family in 1846–7 to designs by Mr Brearley of Liverpool. It was said to have been built 'embracing all the features of a much larger building, and avoiding its defects, covering many square yards, not one foot of which is lost without a use, while the whole edifice is a complete idea, uniform and imposing in its proportions'.

Old Hatfield Court was described in 1876 as 'a picturesque house in the Elizabethan style; it is in ruins and covered with ivy.' The photograph, taken not many years later, shows it to have lost most of its ivy. It has since been pulled down.

Eye Vicarage and Church, c. 1890. Several smaller, but substantial, houses became vicarages, and the most important is that at Eye, some three miles north of Leominster. It was built as a manor house by Ferdinando Gorges, a slave trader, in 1680 and its plain exterior hides some rich plasterwork and panelling. Its external appearance has been changed by the addition of three dormers.

This, and the following photographs of Eye, were taken during the Sandford's residence, sometimes after the Second World War.

Ferdinando Gorges' dining hall at Eye.

The 'Great Parlour' at Eye.

The writing room at Eye.

Five

Uniformed services

Left: centre figure, front row: Head Constable Johnson. *Right:* centre figure, front row
Superintendent Strangward.

LEOMINSTER

MUNICIPAL BOROUGH.

The Proposed Amalgamation of the Borough & County Police.

So much misapprehension appears to exist in regard to the effect of the union of the Borough and County Police, the principle of which received the sanction of the Town Council in August last, that it seems necessary to put the Burgesses in possession of the facts of the case.

The Borough Police consists of a Superintendent, a Sergeant, and six Officers who are responsible to the Watch Committee and to the Borough Magistrates. Their beats extend over the Borough and Out-Parish. There are also two Lock-ups, one belonging to the Borough and the other to the County, at which last a County Superintendent is stationed.

The annual cost of the Borough Police, as shewn in the published accounts, has been on the average of the five years ending August 31st, 1870, £524 18s. 0d.—the average amount of the Government Grant for the same period has been £120 17s. 8d.,—shewing the *nett* annual cost of the Police to have been £404 0s. 4d. There has however recently been an increase of one shilling per week in the wages of the six constables which will raise the present nett cost of the Police Force to about £420 a year. Of this amount the Borough pays almost exactly one half and the Out-Parish the other half.

If the proposed Amalgamation be carried out, a legal agreement will be made between the Borough and the County, by which the County will agree to place at the disposal of the Borough Authorities a certain number of men for whom the Borough will pay at a fixed rate per man. The details of the agreement are not yet finally arranged, but the Government Inspector of Police has intimated that he shall not require a Force exceeding six men, and the Chief-Constable is prepared to find the men at about £51 each, or £306 for the six men per annum. *Either party will be at liberty to terminate the agreement on giving such notice as may be agreed upon.*

These figures show a clear gain to the Municipal Borough of more than £100 a year under the Amalgamation. The Borough is not now, and will not, become liable to the County Police Rate, or to any Police expenses beyond what may be provided for in the agreement, and the respective powers and jurisdictions of the Borough and County Magistrates will be in no way affected thereby.

The Amalgamation of Police has already taken place in many Districts and Boroughs, and its operation has been found satisfactory and economical to both parties. No Borough or County which accepts the Government Grant in aid of Police expenses can be said to retain the control entirely in its own hands. A reduction in the number of men could not be made here without incurring an almost certain loss of the Government Grant. The citizens of Hereford have recently tried the experiment to their cost. And it is very probable that Amalgamation may be made compulsory wherever the Government Grant is given, and that it must then be effected on less favourable terms.

JOHN T. SOUTHALL,
MAYOR.

1, *Corn Square, Leominster.*
October 21st, 1871.

S. PARTRIDGE, PRINTER, BROAD STREET, LEOMINSTER.

This notice refers to the first attempt at uniting the Borough and County Police. The County Police Station was in Burgess Street and the Borough Police Station and Gaol was in New Street.

The actual amalgamation of the Borough and County Police took place in 1889, this photograph being the last ever taken of the Borough force. From left to right, back row: PCs Rooke, Thomas, Crump, Blunsdon, Daymond, Williams. Front row: Sgt McNaught and the imposing figure of Head Constable Johnson. The following is taken from a contemporary newspaper account of Johnson's career: 'In August, 1841, at the age of 13 years, he joined HM ship, 'Volge', 26-gun corvette, at Chatham, and went on the West India and North America stations, returning home about two years later transporting troops from Halifax and Nova Scotia. He remained on the home station in Ireland, and left the 'Volge' at Queenstown in 1844, and joined the Government troopship 'Apollo'. In this he made two voyages out to Quebec and St John's, Newfoundland, one to Malta and the Ionian Islands, with troops. He was laid off from this ship in 1845, and enlisted later that year into the Chatham Division of Royal Marines, being drafted with a party as supernumeraries on board HM ship, 'Trafalgar', 120 guns, in the spring of 1846, and cruised with the Channel squadron during the summer months under Commodore Collier, till the squadron broke up, and he returned to barracks again. In the spring of 1847 he was sent with a party of supernumeraries, as before, on board HM ship, 'The Howe', 120 guns, under Vice-Admiral Sir William Parker. The fleet ran into Gibraltar where he was drafted on board 'The Sidon', steam frigate, in September, 1847. This vessel was ordered home to transport the Earl of Dalhousie and suite to Alexandria, on his way out as Governor-General of India, and brought Sir H. Hardinge from Alexandria to Trieste. He remained on Mediterranean station until 1849, when he was ordered home, and was paid off. He then volunteered for service in the Royal Marine Artillery, in which he remained until November, 1850, and then joined the City of London Police. He resigned that appointment in October 1856, and, after a short interval, joined the East and West India Dock Company's police service, which he left in 1857, when he entered private service, until September 1858. Then he joined the Herefordshire Constabulary as constable, and in 1859, he was promoted to the rank of superintendent of the upper division of Radnorshire. In May 1864, he changed over to the Herefordshire Constabulary again as clerk in the Chief Constable's office, where he remained until he was appointed Head Constable of the borough of Leominster police force on 7 August 1866.'

Leominster Division of the Herefordshire Constabulary, 1893. From left to right, back row: PC 16 Jones, PC 13 Powell, PC 32 Biggs, PC 45 Oakley. Middle row: PC 41 Greenhouse, PC 7 Jeans, PC 2 Thomas, PC 9 Barnett, PC 60 Hackett, PC 3 Titcombe. Front row: Sgt 53 Smith, Sgt 23 Jones, Supt Strangward, Sgt 54 Hyde, Sgt 14 Marston. Superintendent Strangward had been in charge of the Leominster Division in 1889 and had taken over from Head Constable Johnson, who then retired. Mr Strangward was born in Shobdon in 1845 and, at the age of 12, entered the large engine works of the London and North Western Railway at Crewe. Two years later, in 1859, he sailed to North America, landing at New York. He ultimately found work at Troy, about two hundred miles from New York, in some large engineering works where he took charge of the engine. He remained in Troy until 1863 at a time when the country was convulsed by the American Civil War which had begun in the summer of 1861. He sailed home in 1863 and at once obtained the same job in the engine works at Crewe he had left six years before. He remained there for nearly three years, and then left, joining the Herefordshire County Constabulary in 1867 as a constable at Ross. Here he lived for nearly eight years, being promoted to the rank of sergeant. He transferred to Bromyard and then six years later to Malvern, where he lived for two years. In November 1882, he was appointed as superintendent of the county police of the Leominster and Wigmore districts.

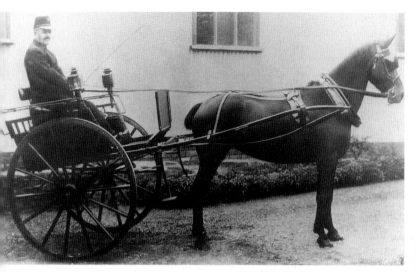

Superintendent Price of Leominster Division, sometime before 1908.

Church Street, probably during the Peace Parade of 1919. Marching from the Town Hall down Church Street, the police, sandwiched between the fire brigade and Borough officers, are just passing the now vanished Baker's Arms.

The funeral of the late Superintendent Groves in 1936.

Sergeant L. Workman outside Leominster police station in Burgess Street, *c.* 1950. This police station with its adjoining magistrates court was built in 1885 on part of the site of the old theatre.

Schedule of Charges & Payments.

ENGINE FREE IN MUNICIPAL BOROUGH OF LEOMINSTER.

	Call.	First 5 hrs' or part of same.	Per hr. after first five
	s. d.	£ s. d.	s. d.
ENGINE— Beyond Boundary, all time to be reckoned from time of Engine leaving station, until its return to same place. One hour for cleaning.		2 2 0	5 0
Captain	5 0	0 5 0	1 6
Engineer	3 6	0 5 0	1 0
Fireman (each)	2 0	0 4 0	0 9
Drivers (each)		0 7 6	0 6
Extra assistance on report of Captain, not to exceed per hour....			0 6
Premium to Fireman who first arrives at Town Hall			2 6

Payment for each Drill of not less than 2 hours :—

Captain	..	..	..	—
Engineer	..	..	..	—
Firemen (each)	..	..	..	1 6

N.B.—The present arrangement for the horsing of the Engine is £1 1s. 0d. per horse.

Where horses not required after call a fee of 10s. at night and 5s. in day will be allowed.

Rules, Regulations, and Instructions.

Rules & Duties of Committee.

(1.)—The Borough of Leominster Fire Brigade shall consist of a Captain, Engineer, and 12 Firemen.

(2.)—The General Purposes Committee of the Town Council to be the sole authority to frame or alter Rules, and to appoint Captain, confirm the appointment of Firemen and Officers, have all financial management, and final power Five to be a quorum.

(3.)—To meet Quarterly, or oftener if necessary, or if requested to do so by five members thereof, and always within a week of the occurrence of any fire which the Brigade shall have attended, to receive the report of the Captain, and consider the same.

(4.)—To frame schedule of charges and revise same when necessary, fix all salaries, receive all monies payable, and make all payments, assess all costs and remunerations, authorise and audit all bills and claims for and against the Brigade.

The 1891 charges and rules for the Leominster fire brigade. Organised fire-fighting in Leominster has a long history going back at least to 1692 when Lord Coningsby gave the town a large fire engine. The charity school-room was built over the engine house in 1720. The Captain of the Brigade in 1891 was Charles E.A. Moore, one of the small children in petticoats on page 30. There had always been some friction between the Borough and the surrounding area with regard to the fire brigade and you will notice that the charges above all refer to 'Beyond Boundary'. The Leominster and Wigmore Rural District had always avoided setting up their own brigade and, after the 1938 Fire Service Act became operative, arrangements were made for the Leominster Borough Fire Brigade to extend its cover to the whole of the rural district. It maintained its independence until 1 April 1948, when it became Station 2 for the County of Hereford Fire Brigade.

Left: Captain C.E.A. Moore. Right: Leominster fire brigade attending a fire in Drapers' Lane.

The brigade after a farm barn fire at the Homme in 1936. The gentleman in the bowler hat is the engineer, Mr J.J. Biddle, landlord of the Chequers Inn, Etnam Street.

The post office moved to Jubilee Buildings in Victoria Street at about the time of the Queen's Golden Jubilee in 1887. It had previously been in Church Street (*c.* 1830), Drapers' Lane (*c.* 1840), the High Street (*c.* 1850), and finally at 18, Broad Street. It served the whole area as the route instructions on the next page show.

ROUTE INSTRUCTIONS.

(To be gummed on the fly sheet of Rural Postman's Rule Book.)

Rural _Foot_ .... *Post from _a_ _____ _____
to ...._._._ _____ .... on ... _N_ _____ ......

OUTWARD JOURNEY.	Hours of Working.		OUTWARD JOURNEY.	Hours of Working.	
	H.	M.		H.	M.
Commence Duty at	0	0	S _____ _____	4	40
Leave Office at	0	30		12	5
Principal places of call			_____ S.O.	4	45
_____ _____				12	10
W _____ _____					
_____ _____					
_____ _____					
_____			_____ L.B.	6	0
_____ _____ ton				1	25
T _____ W _____	8	55			
_____ _____ S.O.	9	0	W _____ _____		
_____ _____					
_____ _____					
_____ _____					
_____ _____ Hut	10	15		1	45
			Arrive ...		10

* Insert { Foot. / Cycle or / Mounted. } | A second sheet should be used where necessary for a second out-and-in journey or for a Sunday journey. Each sheet should be signed by the Postman.

*15m/12/24—[5580] 2943/1507 30m (2) 5/25 8857 G & S **163**

These route instructions, dated 1 January 1921 and signed by postman, W.J. Gatehouse, show the route he had to cover on foot daily and gives the time he was allowed to take. It would be interesting to know the location of the 'shelter hut', and also what he did between 10.15 a.m. and 4.40 p.m.

Six

Leominster railways

Leominster Station in 1900. In 1846 two bills were introduced into parliament containing proposals for constructing a railway between Shrewsbury and Hereford, one proposing to use the broad gauge system, the other the narrow gauge. The latter proposal carried the day. However, with the collapse of the contemporary 'railway mania' nothing was done until 1 January 1851 when work started on the line between Shrewsbury and Ludlow. At the same time work on the Dinmore tunnel, south of Leominster, was begun. The engineer who laid out the line was Mr Henry Robertson, and the contractor Mr Brassey. The line was opened to Ludlow in April 1852, and work was commenced on the Ludlow to Hereford section. The whole line was opened on 5 December 1853. The first locomotive, named the Gipsy Lass made its appearance at Leominster, just north of the Poplands crossing, a few months before the line was opened, creating quite a sensation in the town. Hundreds who had never seen a locomotive in their lives hurried down to see the 'puffing billy'. The early stations seem to have been quite primitive affairs. Hereford station was a hut a few yards south of the Barrs Court bridge, but the most extraordinary station was Moreton. Here there were two famous hollow oaks, named Adam and Eve. Eve was roofed over, and constituted the station, tickets regularly being issued from it.

Dinmore station, showing one of the tunnels. The Shrewsbury to Hereford railway was built as a single track with the idea that the line would soon have to be doubled. For this reason the directors had intended that the Dinmore tunnel should be wide enough for two sets of rails. The engineer, Mr Robertson, however, seems to have differed in opinion on this point and in his specification to the contractor only stipulated for the tunnel to accommodate a single line. The directors did not examine the details of the contract and, until the completion of the tunnel, remained under the impression that they had contracted for a double line. Mr Robertson excused himself by saying 'it is no use spending £20,000 on a double tunnel which can never been wanted', a view supported by Mr Brassey. However, they had not allowed for the great traffic in bunker steam coal that sprang up between South Wales and Liverpool. So, a second tunnel had to be built. The second line was completed in 1893.

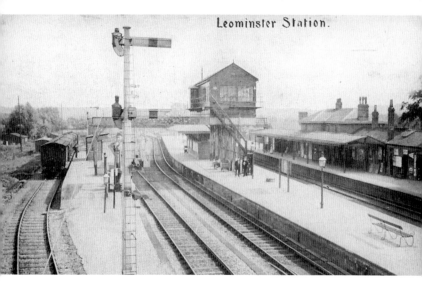

Leominster station showing all five platforms. On Friday 17 February 1865 the following report appeared in the Leominster & Hereford Express under the headline 'Frightful Boiler Explosion': 'About half-past two o'clock on Sunday morning the quiet town of Leominster was roused out of its slumber by a loud report as of an earthquake. On inquiry it was found that a boiler had exploded at the railway station, carrying destruction with it, to replace which will cost the company about £1,000. It appears that the two o'clock luggage train from Hereford arrived at the Leominster station some minutes before its time. The driver and fireman left the train and went to the porter's room, and at about two minutes before the time for again starting the boiler burst with a fearful crash, lowering to the ground the passengers' and Kington carriage sheds on the one side, and on the other knocking nearly the whole of the station building into ruin. The booking office and gentlemen's waiting room were turned completely topsy turvy; the lady's waiting room and the room over it belonging to the station master were destroyed and the roof gone. So narrow was the escape of the station master that had the engine been drawn a yard further, the whole of the domestic portion of the station must have shared the same fate as the waiting rooms. The bookstall, belonging to Mr Partridge, was also demolished, with its contents. To show the immense power of steam, several huge pieces of timber were thrown to the topmost branches of poplar trees, some distance from the station, and a part of the engine itself was thrown some hundreds of yards up Etnam-street. Pieces of timber and iron were scattered in all directions. By the great exertions of the station master and the Superintendent of Police, the obstructed line was soon made available for traffic, the former gentleman telegraphing to Hereford and Shrewsbury for assistance. Mr Paget, with a staff of workmen, went over to the scene of the catastrophe about middle day (Sunday) and we believe that a strict enquiry will be made to ascertain if anyone be in fault. The scene was visited by hundreds of the inhabitants throughout the day.'

Ford Bridge station. The completion of the main line from Newport to Shrewsbury was soon followed by the building of a line between Leominster and Kington, commenced in 1854 and opened in 1857. The line from Kidderminster to Woofferton, however, took a far more considerable length of time to complete being built in stages between 1859 and 1878.

Kingsland station.

LONDON AND NORTH-WESTERN RAILWAY.

MIDSUMMER EXCURSIONS, 1867.

MARCUS'S SPECIAL TRAIN

On MONDAY, JUNE 24th,

Fares for the Double Journey :—

Closed Carriages, First Class,

FROM

HEREFORD at -	- 8 0 a.m.		
LEOMINSTER -	- 8 32 ,,		
TENBURY - -	- 8 10 ,,		
WOOFERTON -	- 8 46 ,,		
LUDLOW - -	- 8 56 ,,	**12s 6d**	**25s**
KNIGHTON - -	- 9 42 ,,		
BUCKNELL -	- 9 50 ,,		
CRAVEN ARMS	- 9 16 ,,		
CHURCH STRETTON	9 35 ,,		

Children under Twelve Years of Age Half-price

TO EUSTON SQUARE STATION,

LONDON,

Returning from the Euston Square Station, London, on THURSDAY, JUNE 27th,

at **9-50** a.m.

Tickets NOT TRANSFERABLE. Luggage under 60 lbs. Free, at PASSENGERS' OWN RISK.
Neither the Company nor Conductor can, in any way, be responsible for detention on the Line; at the same time, EVERY EXERTION will be made to ensure punctuality.

☞ ASK FOR MARCUS'S EXCURSION- TICKETS

Small Bills may be obtained at the " Times " Newspaper Office ; at Messrs. CHAPLIN and HORNE'S, 7, Windmarsh Street, Hereford. Tickets and Bills may be obtained of the Booking Clerks at the above Stations.

HENRY R. MARCUS, Excursion Agent,

6, Slater St., and 25 Leigh St., Liverpool, and 24, Crosby Hall Chambers, 25, Bishopsgate St., London.

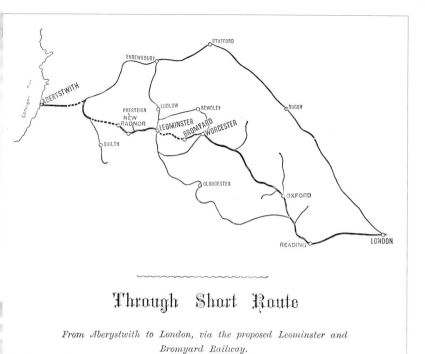

Through Short Route

From Aberystwith to London, via the proposed Leominster and Bromyard Railway.

Some time before the Bromyard railway was finished, there was a proposal to make it part of a new route from mid-Wales (i.e. Aberystwyth) to London. The following letter was sent by R.D. Green Price and Edwin Lloyd on 24 October 1873 in which they wrote: 'It is contemplated to endeavour to carry a Bill for this line through Parliament in the coming Session, as a distinct undertaking from the present Worcester, Bromyard and Leominster Line, and it is desirable that all Land owners and others interested in the making of this important link of communication between Leominster, Worcester and London, should be present to hear the proposals of the Gentlemen who are prepared to assist in the undertaking. We particularly request the favour of your attendance at the Oak Hotel, on Friday the 31st inst., at 3 o'clock in the afternoon for this purpose.' Although the Bromyard-Leominster section was completed, the link between New Radnor and the mid-Wales line north of Builth Wells was not. It would have been far too expensive.

Steen's Bridge station. The construction of the Worcester, Bromyard and Leominster railway proved a real marathon. This was begun in 1874 and the line from Worcester to Bromyard was completed in 1877. Leominster to Steen's Bridge opened in March 1884. There was considerable interest in Leominster in the possibility of a line to Worcester, and a shareholder wrote to the *Leominster News* in September, 1884 asking when the final section of the line would be built. This elicited the following letter: 'Sir, "A Shareholder" asks in last week's *Leominster News* when the directors intend pushing on the line to Bromyard. I might almost be inclined to reply in the words of a well-known comic song, "When pigs begin to fly." But perhaps with the latest introduction of young and vigorous blood into the body directorate we shall see a reformation forcibly reminding us of the times when Mr Alderman Southall did so much for the railway, and for which he was subsequently rewarded with the polite "kick out"'. The letter was signed 'Another Shareholder'. His worst fears were almost justified. Nearly ten years later on 10 October 1893 the following verse 'The Steen's Bridge Railway - A Lament' was published in the same paper:

Another year is well nigh o'er,
And I - am as I was before!
They've told me oft' you're going on,
Till I am sick of that old song,
Why don't they give the final touch?
It would not cost me so very much.
I feel I'm now of litle use,
And get no end of round abuse
Its not my fault; but theirs the blame
Who keep me to the same old game!
Oh! how I long for greater length
To give me greater scope and strength

I should become on opening day,
A public boon – an iron way
To join what's been so long apart,
And crown the wish of many a heart.
Ho! travellers all! around me rally,
With Father Time no longer dally.
Of course the wily Railway Board
Now send you round by Hereford.
And so they will, I greatly fear
Unless you rise and make a stir.
Yes, rise at once, put on the screw.
You'll find that nothing else will do.

The completed line was actually opened on 1 September 1897.

Left: Mr George Child. *Right:* Mrs Child. With a main line and three branch lines, Leominster was an important railway junction. From 1867 to 1900 the station master was Mr George Child; he and his family lived at the station.

Left: Miss Lorna Child. *Right:* George Edward Morris, born 1855.

DALLEY'S
WEST OF ENGLAND RAILWAY TIME TABLES

APRIL, 1899

PUBLISHED BY

F. A. DALLEY

(Late SAXBY)

PRINTER, BOOKSELLER & STATIONER
13 HIGH STREET & 12 DRAPERS' LANE
LEOMINSTER

THE NORTH TO SOUTH WALES AND BRISTOL

(Timetable grid — columns headed a.m. / p.m. throughout, with a SUNDAY section at right.)

Station						
L & Manchester (Exchange)		7 45	7 45	9 40	9 40	1045
W & Liverpool		8 08	8 0	1020	1020	1150
G & Chester		9 00	9 0	1110	1110	1242
Edinborough (Caled.)		1050	1050			
Glasgow (Central)		1045	1045			
Carlisle		1 50	1 50	406	408	30
Preston		6 25	6 25	9 26	9 26	1120
Leeds		6 05	6 0	8 55	8 55	9 50
Liverpool		1155	1155			
Manchester		12 0	12 0			
Crewe		1 20	1 30	3040	3040	1140
SHREWSBURY		2 52	20	1027	1027	1235
London		6 50	6 50	1210		
Birmingham		1051	1051			
Wolverhampton		11 0	11 0	4 0	42 9	0 8 30
SHREWSBURY		12 6	12 6	4 14	4 14	9 10 0
SHREWSBURY dep	2 15	2 35	3 30	6 50	8 25	10 5
Condover			7 08	8 35	1013	
Dorrington			7 17	8 43	1019	
Leebotwood			7 24	8 50	1026	
Church Stretton			7 35	8 57	1031	
Marsh Brook			7 39	9 0	1040	
Craven Arms	1 17		7 49	9 10	1049	
Onibury			7 59	9 10	1055	
Bromfield			8 0	9 25	11 0	
Ludlow	1 20		8 10	9 5	11 6	0
Woofferton Junction			8 15		1145	
Berrington & Eye			8 23	1021		
LEOMINSTER	1 47		8 33	1020		
Ford Bridge			8 40	103		
Dinmore			8 47	1050		
Moreton			8 50	1059		
Hereford, Brs. Ct. ar	3 2	3 13	4 5	8 9	7 11	0
HEREFORD, B. C. dp	3 3	3 13	5 3	7 15	9 15	1052
Train Inn			7 25	9 25		
Pontrilas			7 32	9 42		
Abergavenny			7 52	101		
Pontypool Road			7 55	8 37	1000	1040
dep			8 55	8 37	1000	1040
Newport, High St.	5 5		8 53	9 16	1132	
Cardiff			6 35	9 25	1123	1135
Severn Tunnel Junc.		5 15	7 37	1031	1215	
BRISTOL arr	5 15	7 37	1038	1215		

Mondays only, a Train leaves Craven Arms 4.35, Onibury 4.41, Bromfield 4.46, arriving at Ludlow 4.51.
A Train runs from Woofferton to Le'master daily at 8.12. ‡ Sets down passengers booked through from beyond Shrewsbury
  c Sets down passengers from stations beyond Shrewsbury, and picks up for London.
  t 9.52 Hereford to Cardiff, Mons. only § Calls to set down from Shrewsbury & beyond & to pick up for London.

Leominster, Kington, Eardisley, Presteign, New Radnor

		a.m.	a.m.		p.m	p.m	Sun p.m
LEOMINSTER dep		5 30	9 55	1 0	4 5	5 50	8 45
Kingsland		5 41	10 5	1 11	4 16	5 59	8 54
Pembridge		5 51	1013	1 20	4 24	6 7	8 58
Titley		6 5	1024	1 31	4 37	6 10	9 10
KINGTON ar	6 10	1028		1 36	4 42	6 23	9 13
Kington		9 10	1115	3 25	6 25	
Titley		9 15	1122	3 31	6 30	
Lyon's Hall		9 20	1127	3 39	6 35	
Almeley		9 30	1137	3 51	6 45	
EARDISLEY ar	9 35	1142	3 57	6 50	
Kington dep	6 50	1032	1 20	5 5	6 30	
Titley	6 56	1037	1 32	5 10	6 37	
PRESTEIGN ar	7 10	1050	1 46	5 25	6 50	
Kington dep		1031	1 45	5 5	0*36	
Stanner		1040	1 54	5 14	0 39	
Dolyhir		1045	1 59	5 19	0 44	
NEW RADNOR		1050	2 5	5 25	0 50	

		a.m.	a.m.	p.m	p.m	p.m	Sun p.m
NEW RADN'R dep		1055	2 13	5 50	
Dolyhir		11 1	2 20	5 56	
Stanner		11 5	2 27	6 1	
Kington arr		1118	2 35	8 10	
PRESTEIGN dep	7 20	11 0	2 20	5 45	7 10
Titley	7 30	1125	2 48	6 07	7 24
Kington arr	7 40	1130	2 53	6 17	7 30
EARDISLEY dep	9 55	12 0	4 30	7 10
Almeley	10 0	1210	4 35	7 15
Lyon's Hall	1011	1228	4 46	7 26
Titley	1016	1237	4 51	7 31
Kington arr	1020	1242	4 57	7 35
KINGTON dep	7 50	1113	2 40	6 12	7 45
Titley	7 53	1124	3 48	6 17	7 50
Pembridge	8 5	1131	2 55	6 28	8 5
Kingsland	8 14	1144	3 4	6 38	8 24
LEOMINSTER ar	8 20	1150	3 15	6 48	8 30

BRISTOL AND SOUTH WALES TO THE NORTH Sundays

		a m	a m	a m	a m	a m	a m	9 30	a m	a m	p m	1149	1245	p m	p m	p m	p m	p m		2 20	4 03	3 10	p m	4 25	7 40	5
BRISTOL	dep	1 5																		2 25					5 0	
Severn Tunnel																											
Cardiff		1 30			6 33		9 30						1243		1 82	25		2 40	4 12		5 37	4	307	35
Newport, High Street		1 58			6 56		9 51							1 24	1 38	1 312	48	4 193	3 34		5 32	4	31	5 58	2
Pontypool Road	arr				7 20		1013	1023						2 23		83 26	3	33 5	7		6 58	22		8 42
"	dep				7 34		1029	1031				1040		1 28	1 43	2 73	26		3 38	5 15		4 15	41		8 45
Abergavenny "					8 8							11 8				2 38			4 3		6 40			9 3
Pontrilas					8 40							1141				3 12			4 33		7 12			9 33
Tram Inn					8 57							1159				3 31					7 25			9 59
Hereford, Barrs Ct	ar	2 55			9 10		1117	1117				1213	2 14	2 20	3 45	4	14 4	14 4	57 6	3	7 40	9	272	55 1015
HEREFORD	dep	3 07	30		9 20		1122		1137	1245 2	20	40		3 30 4	20	4 305	156	0	308	0 9	323	6	1010 4	0
Moreton			7 39						1146	1238						4 39	8		6 39				1050	
Dinmore			7 46		9 33				1153	§						4 45 5	28		6 46	8	14		1066 8	14
Ford Bridge			7 53						1159							4 51	8		6 53				1053	
LEOMINSTER		8 0		9 47				12 6	1252				3 52		4 585	42		7 0	8 27			11 0	8 27
Berrington and Eye		8 7	8					1212						5 45	49		7 6				11 7	
Woofferton Junction		8 15	10 2					1219 1	4			4 6		5 115	57		7 158	35			1114 8	39
Ludlow		8 279	50 1015					1231 1	14			4 17		5 256	9		7 228	51			1124 8	51
Bromfield		8 339	55	8				1238						5 29 6	14		7 30				1130 9	50
Onibury		8 399	10	8				1244						5 346	20						1137	
Craven Arms		8 48 10	7	1035				1255 1	35		3 30 4	35	5 396	30		9 8				1145 9	9
Marsh Brook		8 58 1015					1 1													1150	
Church Stretton		9 8 10231052					1 9				3 45 4 51					9 26				12 0 9	22
Leebotwood		9 15 1035					1 16						3 57							12 9	
Dorrington		9 23 1045					1 22						3 57							1215	
Condover		9 31 1042					1 27				4 6									1220 9	34
SHREWSBURY	arr	4 09 40 1050 1113			1230		1 40 2	53 4	8		4 15 5 10 5	28		7 0 7	18		9 47 10 04			1210 9	47
SHREWSBURY	dep	7 25 10 0	11 7		1 33		2 15			4 25		5 50													
Wolverhampton		8 45 1042 1146			2 13		3 25			5 15		7 5										1017 8	35
Birmingham		9 20 11 7 1215			2 38		3 52			5 40		7 43										1059 9	32
London			2 53 3	30		5 20		7 35			8 45		1045										2 20	
SHREWSBURY	dep	4 50	9		1150		1235		2 184	54	5	10 5	35		7 20			8			10 5 1059	4 51	0 10 5
Crewe		4 45 1018		1250		1 25		3 203	29 4	43	6 10 6	17		7 55				11 11	1143 4	52 211	1
Manchester		5 50			2 15		4 30		4 305	20 5	51		7 15		9 30						5 55 5	04 1	5
Liverpool		6 10 1115		2 0		2 40		4 504	50 5	50		7 25		9 20						1206 6	0 5	3 10
Leeds		8 53 1	8	4 20		4 20		4 50 6	10 7	10		1035		1110				5 47 1219	2	5 47
Preston		6 10 1235		1 58		3 15		5 425	42 6	25		7 35			1022			2 12 10 10 1	4 0 2	12
Carlisle		8 50 3	5	3 55		5 48		6 15											2 12 4	8	8 18 3	3
Glasgow (Central)		1210 5	0	6 20		8 26		1030												6 43		6 43
Edinboro' (Caledon)		1255 5	0	6		8 20		1050												6 34		6 39

G.W.R.

Chester		5 50 1130 1235		1235		1 50 1	50 3	33 3	33 4	59		7 2		7 20			8 33				1238 5	50 6	45
Liverpool		6 29 1230 01	30	1 30		3 03	04 4	04 4	36 6	0		8 0		8 10			9 25				6 26 9	50
Manchester Ex.		9 16 1252 3	2	3 2		4 12 4	125	105	106	12		8 37		8 57			1010				9 35 5	50

‡ Stops to pick up passengers * Stapleton Road § Calls to set down passengers from stations beyond Hereford
Mondays only, a train leaves Woofferton Junct. for Ludlow at 11.35; also Ludlow for Craven Arms at 2.50
A train leaves Woofferton Junction daily for Ludlow at 7 p.m, also Craven Arms for Shrewsbury at 7 p.m.

TENBURY AND BEWDLEY LINE, G.W.R. (Week days)

	a m	a m	a m	a m	9 50	a m a m	p m	p m	p m	p m			a m	a m		p m p m	p m p m
PADDINGTON	...	...	...	...	...		1 40	1 45			LEOMINSTER	6 50	8	0	...	9 47 ...	3 52 5 42 7	0
Worcester	...	7 20	...	9	45	1257	...	5 49	6 30		LUDLOW	6 50 8	4	...	10 5 1134 4	15 6 53 ...
Wolverhampton	7 20	...	8	39 12	3	12 0	...	5 53 5	48		Woofferton	7 8	45	...	1020 1135 4	40 7 15 7115
Birmingham	7 10	...	9	2	11	01235	...	4 33 5	58		Easton Court	7 16 8	55	...	1025 12 0 4	47 20 7120
BEWDLEY	8 51	...		10 33	2	3 2	3	...	5 49 7	25		Tenbury	...	7 23 9	2 9*	45 1033 1212 4	56 7 25 7125
Wyre Forest	9 2	...		10 48	2 14	2 14	...	6 0	7 36		Newnham	7 32		...	9 53 1041 1220 5	5
Cleobury Mort.	9 9	...		10 56	2	12 21	...	6 5	7 43		Neen Sollars	7 39		...	9 59 1047 1226 5	12
Neen Sollars	9 17	...		11 4	2	28 2 28	...	6 17	7 50		Cleobury Mort.	7 50		...	10 9 1058 1226 5	24
Newnham	9 23	...		11 9	2	34 2 34	...	6 23	7 56		Wyre Forest	7 56		...	1015 11 4 1243 5	30
TENBURY	7 50 9	40 9	40	11 18	3	45 3 45 5	30 6	38 8	5		BEWDLEY	8 7		...	1026 1116 1253 5	42
Easton Court	7 58 9	48 9	48	11 25	3	51 3 51 5	38 6	45 8	11		Birmingham	9 40		...	1240 2 30 7	13
Woofferton	arr.	8 5 9	55 9	55	11 30	3	56 3 56 5	46 6	53 8	17		Wolverhampton	9 53		...	1 2 2 50 7	20
LUDLOW	...	8 27 1015 1015		1238 4	17 4	17 6	0	7 10 8	51		Worcester	8 52		...	1120 1240 ... 6	31
LEOMINSTER	...	8 30 1027 1027		11 55 1165 1165 6	45 7	16 8	29			PADDINGTON	1215		...	2 53 ... 5 20 1045

*Runs every Tuesday and alternate Mondays only. §Foregate Street. †Mondays 11.43. :Mondays & Fridays only.

LEOMINSTER & WORCESTER LINE--G.W.R. (Week days only)

		a m	a m	p m p m	p m p m					a m	a m	p m p m	p m p m p m
LONDON (Padd.)	dep		5 40	9 50	1 40 4 45	...		LEOMINSTER	dep.	7 20	8 55	1230 3 57	... 7 45
WOR'STER (Sh'b Hill)	"	8 20	1030	2 40 5	10 8 0	...		Steens Bridge	"	7 31	9	6 12 41 4	8 7 56
(Fore'gte St.)	"	8 23	1033	2 43 5 13 8	3	...		Fencote	"	7 40	9 21 1251 4	17	8 5
Henwick	"	8 28	1038	2 48 5 18 8	8	...		Rowden Mill	"	7 47	9 28 1258 4	24	8 12
Leigh Court	"	8 38	1048	2 58 5 28 8	25	...		Bromyard	{ arr.	7 54	9 35 1 4 4	31	8 19
Knightwick	"	8 45	1055	3 5 5 35 8	25	...			dep.	7 59	9 50 1 20 4	33	8 42
Suckley	"	8 49	1059	3 9 5 39 8	29	...		Suckley	"	8 11	10 2 1 32 4	48	8 54
Bromyard	{ arr.	9 1	1111	3 20 5 51 8	41	...		Knightwick	"	8 15	10 6 1 36 4	49	8 58
	{ dep.	9 4	1114	3 22 5 54 8	44	...		Leigh Court	"	8 22	1013 1 43 4	56	9 5
Rowden Mill	"	9 12	1122	3 30 6	2 8 52	...		Henwick	"	8 31	1022 1 52 5	4	9 13
Fencote	"	9 20	1133	3 39 6	13 9	0	...		Steens Bridge	"	8 35	1026 1 55 5	8	9 17
Steens Bridge	"	9 29	1140	3 46 6 20 9	10	...		WOR'STER (Fore'gt St.)	"	8 37	1027 1 57 5	10	9 19
LEOMINSTER	"	9 37	1148	3 54 6 28 9	18	...		(Sh'b Hill)	ar.	8 40	1031 2 0 5	16	9 22
								LONDON (Padd)	"	1215	2 33 5 50 8	45	

Bookstall at Leominster station, 1890s.

Leominster station, 1950s. In 1901 Leominster got a new signal box between platforms 2 and 3.

Looking north from the signal box, 1950s.

Looking south from the signal box, 1950s. With the exception of the main Shrewsbury & Hereford line, all the railways passing through Leominster have gone, together with three of the platforms and the signal box. Parts of the Leominster & Kington line were closed to passenger traffic in 1951 and the rest in 1955. Freight traffic ceased later, and on 28 September 1964 the line was finally closed completely. The Worcester, Bromyard and Leominster railway had closed three weeks earlier. The Tenbury–Woofferton line closed on 31 July 1961, one day short of its hundredth birthday. All the small stations on the main line, Moreton & Eye, Ford Bridge, Dinmore, etc. have closed. Many of the buildings have survived, however, together with bridges and stretches of embankment belonging to the branch lines; all are now memorials to a bygone age.

Seven

'Creeping like a snail' – Leominster's schools

The Boys of Leominster Orphanage.

As was usually the case in medieval times, education in Leominster was in the hands of the Church up to the time of the Reformation. The town lost the services of the three chantry priests when the monastery was dissolved but when Queen Mary granted the town a new charter in 1554 the grammar school was re-established and £20 per annum granted for the payment of two school masters. The school found a home in the old Forbury chapel, built in the late thirteenth century by John Peckham, Archbishop of Canterbury. A charity school, later to be called the National School, was founded in 1720 in a room built over the engine house near the Forbury chapel, and the two schools continued side-by-side for more than a hundred years. Although Leominster Grammar School was originally established as a free school, it was certainly not 'free' in July 1790 when the following advertisement appeared in the Hereford Journal:

'The Rev. Jonathan Williams, A.M., will open his School again on Monday the 27th instant, for the reception of Young Gentlemen designed for the University, the Professions, or the Superior Lines of Business. Their treatment is liberal, and their instruction conducted on a judicious and comprehensive plan.

> Board and Education, £10, per annum
> Entrance £1 1s 0d
> Day Scholars £3 3s 0d'

Revd Williams seems to have run the school at his house, Copper Hall, in South Street, for a time around 1830. He was a curate at Leominster Priory and the author of *The Leominster Guide* published in 1808. His advertisement was probably needed because of the appearance of rival private schools. The list of academies and schools in Pigot & Co's Directory in 1835 was as follows:

Free Grammar School, Church Street - Francis Burlton, master
Morris, Richard, Burgess Street
National School, Church Street – Edward Wells, master
Poulton, Oakley, Corn Market
Powell, Mary, Burgess Street
Raisbeck, William Kemp (gents' boarding & day) Church Street
Rea, Revd Nathaniel, South Street
Slade, Eleanor (ladies' boarding & day) Grange House
Thomas, George, Etnam Street
Wolley, Elizabeth (ladies' boarding & day) Middle Marsh

Grange House Academy, 1880s. The most interesting of the private schools was that established in Grange House, a building on the site of the two semi-detached brick houses in the south-east corner of the Grange. A girls' school in the 1830s, it was taken over by a Mr Samuel Bedee Cooper in the 1840s and became Grange House Academy, a boy's boarding and day school. We are fortunate to have a first-hand account of schooling in those days written by Thomas Smith, who was a pupil there in the 1840s: 'First, I remember going to a dame's school; afterwards I was sent to one kept by a Mr. Charles Reece; here I staid [sic] for some years till a Mr. Cooper opened a boarding school in Leominster, to which I was removed, and soon made progress in learning. My school-boy days present nothing remarkable, except that I imbibed many pernicious ways which tainted my youngling, and which have tended to embitter my life, and which, to my dying day, will be a source of painful remembrance. One thing was that the schoolmaster, though a kind, and in many things an excellent man, yet was a drunkard. The boys would often rejoice when the master was prevented attending to his duties on account of drink, because they were sure of a holiday.' Grange House was later taken over by Mr Cox and became a very reputable school.

Grange House Academy,

Leominster,

October 28th 1875.

Mr. Perry,

TO JAMES COX, A.C.P.;

ASSOCIATE, PRIZEMAN, AND MEMBER OF THE ROYAL COLLEGE OF PRECEPTORS, LONDON (BY EXAMINATION), MID., 1870.

(Vide "Educational Times," Aug., 1870, and "London Daily News," Sept. 26, 1870.)

Nearly two Years Assistant Master at Vale House Academy, London, N.W.; four years English, Writing, and Assistant French Master at the Priory Classical, Mercantile, and Scientific School, Upper Street, Islington, N.; nearly two years Classical and Mathematical Master at Stourpaine House School, near Blandford, Dorset; four years at the Proprietary School and Technical College, Hereford, as French, Drawing, Painting, and Music Master. Engaged for six years while in London, as Private Tutor to City Gentlemen in the evening; has prepared pupils for the Oxford and Cambridge, the College of Preceptors, the Civil Service, the Post-Office, the Clearing House (Euston Square, London), Marlbrough College, Pharmaceutical, and Matriculation Examination of the London University.

	£	s	d
To One Quarter's Tuition for Masters T & J. P. Pudge			
ending Michaelmas 1875		2	5	0
Drawing 2 9d Stationery Drill 1 9 9/6 &c Bk 6d Atlas 4 Printing 6d		17	0
C. P. Bk 9 2 Cocked Caps 9 Parsing 6d Photograph 4 Pencil Box 9		5	6
Ciphering Bk & Copybooks 9		2	0
	£3	9	6

Received with thanks
November 5 · 1875
James Cox A.C.P.

With Mr & Miss Cox's kind Compts.

Bill for school fees at Grange House Academy in 1875. Note Mr Cox's C.V.

PRINCIPAL:—Mr. JAMES COX, A.C.P.;

(Associate and Prizeman of the Royal College of Preceptors.)

Report of *Master R. E. Bateman*

Christmas 78

SUBJECT	NO. OF MARKS	CLASS	PLACE	REMARKS
SCRIPTURE	500	10	3rd	
ENGLISH GRAMMAR	615	20	1st	
COMPOSITION, &c.	625	10	1st	
HISTORY	525	10	6th	
GEOGRAPHY	552			Master Bateman was
ARITHMETIC	619	5	3rd	successful in attaining
MENTAL CALCULATION	500	10	8th	Prize for
TABLES				Regular Attendance
LAND SURVEYING				Salem (1 Class)
ALGEBRA				J. C.
EUCLID				Xmas 1878
BOOK-KEEPING	519	20	3rd	
WRITING	1161	10	4th	
READING, &c.	314	10	5th	
DICTATION				
LATIN	326	5	1st	
FRENCH				
GREEK				
MUSIC	60	10	7th	
DRAWING Free	10	20	10th	
TOTAL NO. OF MARKS =	8241	CONDUCT.		Good

No. of Times present during Half-year = 17   Late 0   Absent 0

GRANGE HOUSE ACADEMY, LEOMINSTER

This Certificate of Merit

was awarded to

William George Lewis of Haringstone

for general good conduct and improvement in his Scholastic Studies

James Cox, A.C.P.   Principal.

Christmas 1878

MRS. WELLS'S

Establishment for Young Ladies,

[manuscript insertion]

~~LIGHT~~-HOUSE, LEOMINSTER.

Terms:

Board and Tuition in the usual branches of Education,
Twenty-Two Pounds per Annum.

Under Ten Years of Age	18	Pounds per Annum.
~~Weekly Boarders~~	16	do.
Day Boarders	8	do.
Day Pupils	4	do.
Do. under 8 years of age	2	do.

EXTRAS.

Music	4	do.
French	4	do.
Dancing	4	do.
Singing	4	do.
Drawing	4	do.

Wax Flowers and Ornamental Leather Work on the usual Terms.
Laundry Two Pounds per Annum.

Each Young Lady to be provided with Knife and Fork, Spoon, One Pair of Sheets, and Six Towels.

THREE MONTH'S NOTICE REQUIRED PREVIOUSLY TO THE REMOVAL OF A PUPIL.

PAYMENTS QUARTERLY.

This school seems to have been founded in the Lighthouse (see p. 101), Middle Marsh, in the 1850s by Edward Wells who was later joined by his wife Jane. Mr Wells was also accountant and clerk to the Gas Company. Mrs Wells carried on the school after her husband's death, moving to South Street about 1878, when this modified prospectus was issued. However, the school does not seem to have survived long after this date.

The National School. A National Infant School was opened in 1848 in the Priory buildings by Revd G.A. Rogers, Vicar of Leominster. The Free Grammar School had effectively ceased to function before 1840, and the National School had taken over the Forbury chapel. The National schools were firmly Church of England institutions and so in 1853 the non-conformists and Quakers opened a 'British school' in South Street. This moved to the Odd Fellows' Hall in 1859 and to new buildings in Bargates in 1862. Meanwhile, in 1858, new buildings for the National School were opened. A contemporary account describes them as 'a pretty pile of stone buildings near the church...[consisting] of a master's house, and three capacious and separate apartments for boys, girls and infants'.

A boys class at the National School, before the First World War.

British School children, early in the twentieth century.

The final blows to the grammar school were the sale of the Forbury chapel in 1860 and the decision by the Borough to stop the £20 payments, although, after many objections, the latter decision was later reversed and the money paid to the National School. The National and British schools continued their separate ways until 1918 when the British School became the Infants, and the National School the Senior and Junior schools.

One of the early headmasters of the Senior School was Mr A.N. Burkett, seen here with the pupils of 1935.

Leominster Senior School football team, 1927–28 season. That year they were the winners of
the Hereford & District Schools Challenge Cup & League Shield. From left to right, back row:
Mr J.O.R. Hughes, F. Harris, G. Parker, T. Phillips, D. Kimbury, S. Stephen, J. Parker, Mr A.
Jenkins, L. Maund, K. Bruntnell. Front Row: R. Rooke, A. Arrowsmith (Captain), Mr A.N.
Burkett, A. Smith, W. Kent.

Mr Burkett again with the winners of the League Shield, 1930–31 season.

Leominster 'Grammar' School, c. 1910, not long after its opening. Its official title was Leominster Secondary School, not 'Grammar School' as originally advertised. The governors changed their minds about the name because by so doing they would be able to attract grants for the school from the Board of Education.

Pro Patria.

Leominster Grammar School
Athletic Sports, 1918.

2nd Prize Arithmetic Race (Girls over 14)

Won by Frances May Taylor

who gave the value of the Prize to the Fund for
providing food for our Soldiers and Sailors
who are Prisoners of War.

Henry F. Russell *Chairman of the Governors.*

W. R. G. Drennan *Headmaster.*

The centre portion of the school photograph taken in November 1920. The gowned figure in the midst of the staff is W.St.G. Drennan, MSc, the first headmaster of Leominster Grammar School.

Leominster Grammar School – Silurian House, 1921. From left to right, top row: B. Hartley, E. Price, M. Bee, E. Law, P. Drennan, D. Hancorn, C. Parry, G. Price. Second row: W. Morrow, E. Arrowsmith, V. Owens, F. Larcombe, C. Rogers (house captain), D. Bateman, E. Perry, M. Davies. Third row: M. Pounds, M. Pugh, G. Napper, Miss Church (headmistress), N. Thompson, R. Price, G. Smart. Bottom row: J. Rogers, W. Jenny, D. Harvey, M. Davies, P. Craddock, M. Taylor, P. Dunning, O. Davies.

Aerial photograph of the Grammar School, probably taken soon after 1945.

Leominster Grammar School cricket team, 1937. Among those pictured are Bob Morris, Ken Scandrett, Brian Dale, H. Jones, R. Bird, C. Bramfitt, -?- Childs, R. Mainwaring, -?- Howard, S. Perkin, -?- Howard.

Leominster's was not the only grammar school in the area. Weobley had one but the photograph above is of the Old Grammar School, Eardisland. It is still there, now much restored, with the whipping post still just below the end window.

Left: Whipping post, Old Grammar School, Eardisland. *Right*: Bodenham School House before the bellcote was removed in 1971.

The pupils of Dilwyn School with Mr Trembath who was headmaster here from 1884 to 1904.

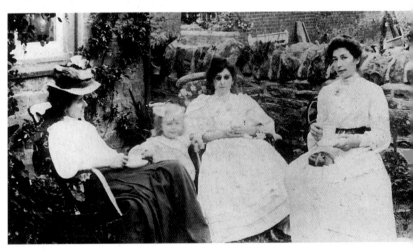

Teacher's wives at tea in the garden of the School House, Kingsland, 1908. *Left:* Mrs Hankinson, with daughter Doris (wife of the head of the British School in Leominster). *Centre:* Mrs Wood (wife of the head of Eardisland School). *Right:* Mrs Knott (wife of the head of Kingsland School).

Eight

The changing face of Leominster

A view few people recognise although all but one of the buildings is still there. The building on the left is the Lighthouse, still there on the north bank of the Kenwater, but the next building, 'The Dingle', is now the entrance to the Broad Street car park. The 'Old House', as it was then known, has acquired bay windows on the ground floor. The photograph was probably taken in the mid-1870s when Ann Footitt is recorded as the licensee of the Bird in Hand public house.

Left: Church Street, Leominster. The removal of the Old Town Hall and the erection of the new one completely changed the view down Church Street. This photograph shows that the shop to the left of the Town Hall where the painter John Scarlett Davis was born, still belonged to the Davis family, in this case either John's brother, Francis, or his nephew.

Below: Church Street looking east, c. 1887.

The removal of the Old Town Hall opened up the view down the High Street, and also opened it up to more traffic. Between the wars this was a two-way street with buses.

Not much change occurred over the years apart from the removal of the gas lamp and the addition of the war memorial and, of course, the arrival of the car.

View from near the north end of Broad Street, looking south, *c.* 1870.

Broad Street, looking south, *c.* 1885. The trees had been planted in 1881 by Alderman T.B. Stallard, the Mayor, to commemorate the holding of the annual Herefordshire Agricultural Society Show in Leominster. The photographer, R. Jones, has gone far enough north to include his shop on the left (see p. 9).

Not the usual traffic hazard in nineteenth-century Broad Street.

An unusual photograph for its time, taken in Broad Street, probably in 1911.

The AC (not yet the RAC) rally driving south on Broad Street, *c.* 1905.

Broad Street, Leominster.

No sign of cars in this picture, although it was probably taken as late as 1909.

The Midland Bank, a 'modern' gas lamp and pollarded trees, Broad Street, *c.* 1930.

Progress at last? No gas lamp, no trees, and cars.

Leominster's Victorian town hall disappeared in stages. First the tower was removed because it was unsafe, and then the roof. Finally, as these two photographs taken in 1975 show, it was reduced to a single story and then removed, leaving the market-hall exposed (see p. 116).

Drapers' Lane is one of the few parts of Leominster which has not changed much over the years. You have to look carefully at the shop-signs and the costumes to tell the approximate date of this photograph – 1900.

High Street looking north, showing the new building built in 1885 on the corner of Victoria Street.

The High Street from the Iron Cross, c. 1905.

Above: When the Post Office moved to Corn Square, Mr Scudamore moved into 2, Victoria Street (see p.71).

Right: The north-west corner of Corn Square before the new Corn Exchange was built in 1859. This replaced the 1808 Corn Market which stood in the middle of the square.

The new Corn Exchange between 1859 and 1885, when Victoria Street was built.

Corn Square after the creation of Victoria Street. This 1920s photograph shows the market in full swing. The odd looking windows on the extreme right seem to belong to an omnibus which used the square as its terminus.

W. E. RODGERS

Formerly trading as GOLDINGS

19 West St., Leominster

Pioneers in the Regular Service of the Daily
Necessaries of the Home to your Door.

HOUSE FURNISHER, OIL MERCHANT & GENERAL PROVIDER

All kinds of
Table and
Hanging
LAMPS

LANTERNS
CHIMNEYS
and
ACCESSORIES

Heating and
Cooking Stoves
and
Crockery Ware

AT YOUR SERVICE
BUSY MORNING SCENE AT
19. WEST STREET.

The CHRISTMAS SEASON

Is a time for replenishing one's household needs, and adding to life's little comforts. It is there where we are of service, for our assortment is of the utility type, with everything for home and household—whether the floor, ceiling, walls or shelves, or the room itself—think of what these require and then visit us.

Floor Coverings	Tea Sets	Rawlplugs
Wallpapers	Pudding Basins	Mirrors
Mattings	Foot Warmers	Coal Buckets
Rugs	Tables, Chairs	Fire Shovels
Bedsteads	Fenders	Baking Pans
Mattresses	Chests of Drawers	Pocket Knives
Children's Cots	Toilet Pairs	Table Cutlery
Toilet Sets	Sideboards	Food Choppers

Advertisement for the firm of W.E. Rodgers, 19, West Street, 1925. It later went back to being Goldings; now sadly missed.

West Street, c. 1910. This part of West Street has not changed much except that the Talbot Hotel has now swallowed up the adjourning premises.

George Page and his father Thomas before him, occupied 21, West Street from the middle of the nineteenth century. The buildings have now been demolished.

Looking east along West Street, *c.* 1930. Several of the buildings on the right were demolished to make an entrance to the car park.

Hester Clarke's 1736 almshouses in Bargates being pulled down for rebuilding in 1874. According to an account written in 1792 the husband of the foundress was remarkable for giving away the best part of his effects during his lifetime. Hence the rhyme inscribed on the building: 'He that gives away before he is dead, let 'em take this Hatchet and knock him on ye head'.

The rebuilt almshouses, c. 1880.

New Street. The whole of the right-hand (south) side was demolished, including the old Borough Gaol, to create the relief road, opened in 1974.

Burgess Street looking east. The large building on the corner is the Town Hall, with the market behind. Taken between 1950, when the Town Hall tower was demolished, and 1975.

The view from Mill Street to the Priory taken early in the twentieth century is an unfamiliar one in many ways. The building on the left is Porter's Mill, which gave its name to Mill Street and the water in the foreground is part of the mill pond. The path by the stream was a favourite with lovers and was called Paradise. The mill, the water, and the path, have all vanished, but not the names.

More water that has disappeared – the Pinsley – seen here flowing along Vicarage Street, *c.* 1910.

The Church Institute lay behind the Friends' Meeting House in South Street. This photograph was taken soon after it was erected in 1906. It was an iron building and contained reading and billiard rooms and a lecture hall. This was where the play mentioned on page 123 was performed. It was pulled down in the late 1960s to make way for the British Legion.

High Street and South Street run left to right on this aerial photograph taken in about 1923. Etnam Street is the prominent street leading to the top right-hand corner. The Church Institute is almost in the centre of the photograph at the corner of the allotments.

Nine

Fun and games

The back of this photograph is inscribed 'To Mr. Beel, Assistant Scoutmaster. In memory of the Scout "Jamboree" of 1920. We shall never forget it! Neither shall we forget your geniality and kindness to us all. From your friend, Henry Gosling, Hon. Scoutmaster'.

Leominster FC. J. Nicholas (goal-keeper), J.H.K. Williams and W. Reynolds (backs),
W. Gough, P. Ingram and H. Lee (half-backs); J.H. Davis (Captain) and T.J. Perks (right-wing);
M.N. Asterley and T. Jones (left-wing); G. Bassett (centre). On Friday 30 March 1888 this article
appeared in the 'Football Notes' section of the *Leominster News*:

'The final for the Herefordshire Cup, has passed off in a most unsatisfactory manner for
all concerned. There cannot be the slightest doubt in the mind of any impartial person, who
witnessed the match, that Leominster won the game on their merits; but were robbed of it by
the imbecile, or wilful unfairness of the referee. Mr. W. Jones of Hereford who was appointed
umpire for Leominster, and several of the team, appealed for a goal which they unquestionably
got, the referee however, was too far up the field... This was in great contrast to the hasty
manner in which he allowed the Ludlow goal. The ball had scarcely passed the posts, before he
declared it a goal, although the referee's decision is not required unless the umpires fail to agree.
However, in this case they both held a different opinion to what he did, yet when appealed to
for a foul, he refused to alter his decision.

The unpopularity of the Ludlowites with the Hereford people led to an unpleasant and
disgraceful scene... A tent was pushed over in the crush, which was followed by several free
fights. Although the Ludlowites were so sanguine of success, as to have two bands and a dinner
in readiness for them, they have not themselves to thank for the result.'

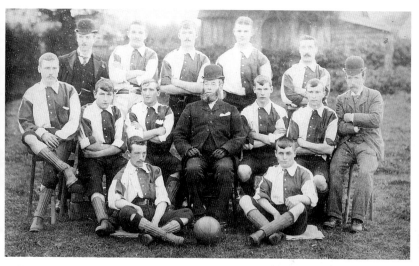

Leominster Town Football Club, 1892–93 season. From left to right, back row: A. Mapp (linesman), W. Fox, J. Phillpotts, B. Cunninghame. C. Holroyd (Captain). Front row: W. Reynolds, H. Clayton, A. Williams, Alderman J. Page, Esq. (Mayor), A. Bassett, T. Jones, G.H. Bourton (Hon. Secretary). Seated on ground: A. Greenhouse, W. Morris. Football was a popular sport in Leominster and, as the photograph shows, received the support of the Mayor, Alderman Page.

Leominster Junior Early Closers, 1906–7 season.

Football was certainly not the only sport practised in Leominster. Here, it looks as though the brewery team won the tug-of-war during the 1897 celebrations surrounding the Diamond Jubilee of Queen Victoria.

Another sport was swimming, especially after the pool in the river north of the town was supplanted in 1939 by these smart new baths in Sydonia.

Entertainment of another kind was provided by the visit of C.S. Kent, the aviator, in March 1927. Flights from Easters were 5/- (shillings) each but one boy secured a free ride by winning a competition for the one who could pull the ugliest face. The newspaper reported that the pilot was a man of iron nerve and was none the worse for having to judge the competition!

Two years before, in January 1925, the Leominster Playfolk put on the play David Garrick at the Leominster Institute. The cast included Mr T.H. Edwards, Mr W.St.G. Drennan (headmaster of Leominster Grammar School), Mr Terry Davis, Miss Eileen Bradford, Miss Peggy Hammond and Miss Winifred Trewin.

Every important national occasion was celebrated in Leominster and this photograph taken from the Corn Exchange shows part of the celebrations for Queen Victoria's Golden Jubilee on 21 June 1887. The local militia are parading in the background while, in the foreground are the Leominster Cyclists, with an impressive array of penny-farthings and tricycles. Note the two gentlemen in their straw 'boaters' riding a 'Sociable'.

Japanese Café at the YWCA Institute. A newspaper report under the headline 'Novel and Attractive Effort' read as follows:

'The Japanese Café, held at the Y.W.C.A. Institute on Wednesday and Thursday, was a novel and happy idea, and it was happily carried out. The effort, with its varied arrangements, must have involved considerable time and labour, but under the spell of its purpose officers and members worked con amore and nothing was left undone that might spell success. The interior of the Institute, with its Japanese decorations, presented a charming appearance. The lower room had been arranged for the concerts three of which were held each day but it was of course in the upper room, where the café had been arranged, that the most delightful transformation had taken place. The decorations, the arrangement of the small tables, each with its menu, were much admired, and the refreshments provided were thoroughly enjoyed. The arrangements were under the supervision of Mrs Johnson, Mrs H.G. Griffiths, and Miss Shelton (who is giving pleasing evidence of her special fitness for the secretarial work of the Association), and these ladies were assisted by a number of the members. There was no lack of help on the two days, the ladies, in their pretty Japanese costumes, including Mrs H. Reynolds, Miss Colwell, Mrs Johnson, Mrs H.G. Griffiths, Miss Watkins, Miss Brace, Miss N. Powell, Miss Hinton, Mrs Storr Barber, Miss Williams, Miss A. Colwell, Miss Bowen, Miss A. Foster, Miss O. Mills, Miss C. Price, Miss I.M. Jones, Miss Cole, Miss J. Ross, Miss L. Freeman, Miss W. Jenkins, Miss Ruddle, Miss B. Weaver, and the Hon. Secretary, Miss Shelton.

Miss Newman presided at the opening of the first concert on Wednesday afternoon at 3.30, when the lower room was crowded. Explaining that the object of the effort was to help the funds of the Association in meeting the expenses of the rooms, she said it was always a pleasure to help those who were doing all they could to help themselves. Such an effort, therefore, commended itself to them and she hoped it would be successful.'

Maureen Davies, Judith Lee Thomas and Mrs Maddox (headmistress) leading the VJ Day fancy-dress parade, August 1945. They were entertained to tea in the 'New Exchange Building' in the background.

Although Leominster has had a 'Picture House' in the Corn Exchange since 1912, the opening of the Clifton Cinema on 31 October 1936 was a cause for celebration. *Escape Me Never* was the film shown for the opening performance, the proceeds going to the Cottage Hospital.

A reminder that Leominster is, and always has been, a market town which depends on the agricultural products of the surrounding area. Hops were, and still are, produced near Leominster, although hop picking as a family 'holiday' is a thing of the past.

Leominster also manufactured goods for the agricultural market, as this product of the Vulcan Works in West Street shows. The photograph was probably taken in the 1880s.